The Economics of Place:

The Value of Building Communities Around People

Edited by Colleen Layton, Tawny Pruitt & Kim Cekola

Published by the Michigan Municipal League
1675 Green Road, Ann Arbor, MI 48105
www.mml.org

"The best way to predict
your future is to create it."

-Abraham Lincoln

Mural of Michigan on the wall of Silvio's Organic Pizzeria, Ann Arbor, Michigan. Courtesy of the Michigan Municipal League

Printed in the United States of America

The League wishes to thank the Michigan State Housing Development Authority (MSHDA) for their assistance in underwriting this book and for its continued support of placemaking initiatives, in particular the Michigan Municipal League's Center for 21st Century Communities. Established in 1966, MSHDA provides financial and technical assistance through public and private partnerships, engaging in community economic development activities to create vibrant cities, towns, and villages, preserve safe and decent affordable housing, and address homeless issues.

Printed by: Printwell, Taylor, Michigan

Book Design by:
genui forma
print design | web media | branding
www.genuiforma.com
Ann Arbor, Michigan

ISBN 978-0-615-47555-4

table of contents

foreword

PETER KAGEYAMA

"Place" shapes us. Place defines us. Place is what forms our identities, our attitudes, and our relationships. Yet we think of place as an externality that is somehow separate from our core identity. Our places are sending us millions of messages, most subconsciously processed, but internalized and felt nonetheless. We don't often think about why we feel comfortable in certain spaces. We just are. We don't think enough about the positive impact of quality places, nor do we measure the negative impact of poor design, ugliness, or banality of our places. But that is changing.

Until recently, we had not thought about how our places made us healthier or happier, yet that is now an emerging aspect of planning. So too is the idea that places drive economic activity. This goes far beyond the idea of creating amenity—rich environments to attract and retain businesses and talent. Placemaking cannot be separated from social, cultural and transportation elements. It must now be seen as setting the fundamental conditions for key drivers such as entrepreneurship, creativity, curiosity, and innovation. Our placemaking policy is now our economic policy and the repercussions of that are huge. ***No longer is it sufficient to build places that are merely functional and safe. Our placemaking aspirations must be as high and as grand as our economic goals because they are bound together.***

For Michigan, this shift in thinking is more critical and perhaps more difficult than in many other places. This is because there is a mythology around Michigan—and Detroit in particular. It is the mythology of the car, of the industrial revolution, of the rise of the American middle class which is written into the DNA of the entire country. Even people who have never been to Michigan and for whom Detroit is a punch line or a cautionary tale understand the mythology. That powerful myth and the narrative that goes with it are very hard to change. Everything we believe about our industrial and manufacturing identity is tied to Michigan. To change that is to change ourselves and that may prove to be the greatest challenge.

Can we think differently about places like Detroit, Flint, and Grand Rapids? Can we challenge all that we thought we knew and consider something radical and different? ***Change is difficult, sometimes even painful and destructive, but change is essential for growth and change must come to all our communities.*** We have Michigan and Detroit ahead of us, leading the way again as they did at the vanguard of the 20th century industrial wave. Today they are leading the next generation of thinking and doing on how places reinvent themselves in the 21st century.

I have been a fan and a supporter of Michigan since my first visit in 2007 at the invitation of the Michigan Cool Cities Initiative. I was shown around the state and saw an amazing array of activities, developments, and people who were deeply committed to, or even in love with Michigan. That is the lesson I carry with me still; ***the people who have chosen to stay in Michigan, to make their stand and stake their claim*** to the future of the community are the most inspirational, resilient, and innovative individuals I have ever met. They have embraced that change, taken the negatives and made them into opportunities. These people will not let Michigan fail. They will not let Detroit die. They ***are the shapers of place, the makers of communities, and the future of our communities.***

I'm sure that you will be inspired by the stories in this book, as well as enjoy learning about the cutting-edge innovation that will make Michigan a great state in the 21st century.

Long Live Michigan!

Peter Kageyama

- Founder: Creative Cities Summit & author, *For the Love of Cities*

introduction

DANIEL GILMARTIN

Culture Front & Center *Zero Emission Public Transit*
Open Source Government
Farm Fresh Food *Venture-Capital Mind Set*
Renaissance Neighborhoods
Incentivized Teachers *Car Sharing* *Smart Energy*

If you thought the preceding list was a preview of the new fall lineup of a Cat Stevens-inspired basic cable channel you would be wrong. The list, in fact, represents the categories that *Fast Company* magazine used recently to depict the best business climates in cities across the country. *Fast Company*, for those not familiar with the publication, describes itself as "dedicated to reporting about how the 'fast companies', entrepreneurs, and cutting edge are doing what they are doing."

If we think that the quality of Michigan's places doesn't play a vitally important role in shaping our economic future, then we better think again.

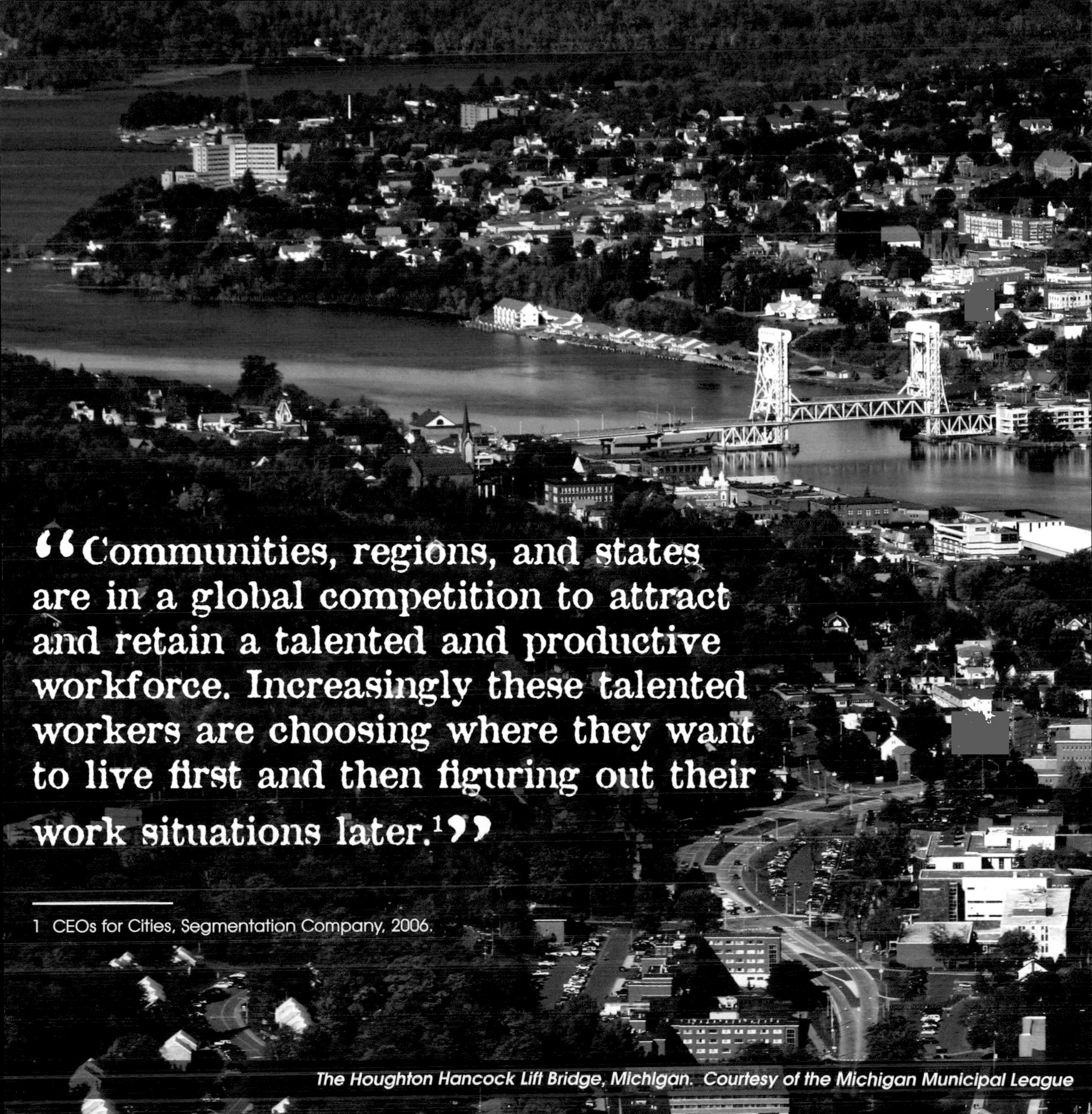

"Communities, regions, and states are in a global competition to attract and retain a talented and productive workforce. Increasingly these talented workers are choosing where they want to live first and then figuring out their work situations later.[1]"

1 CEOs for Cities, Segmentation Company, 2006.

The Houghton Hancock Lift Bridge, Michigan. Courtesy of the Michigan Municipal League

Michigan stands at a crossroad. It's no secret that the methods that we used to build our old economy no longer work in a globally competitive economic environment. Our old economy was built around heavy industry. Protecting and promoting a system that kept corporations like Ford, General Motors, and Chrysler centered in our state was the central theme of most economic development efforts during the 20th century. The common thinking went like this; "these corporate giants provide us a strategic economic advantage over our competitors, so let's make sure we do everything to maintain it." And the plan worked marvelously for a long time, too. If you're bored and looking for something to do, check out the census figures in Michigan from 1930 to 1980. You will find that our state enjoyed an overall prosperity rivaled by few; steady population growth, wages and benefits for workers well above the national average, high homeownership rates—in short, the American Dream. Many historians rightfully credit Michigan and its enormous industrial prowess with helping to solidify the middle class in the United States.

However, as the 20th century moved into its final quarter we began seeing cracks in what many thought was a foolproof foundation for continued growth. The fractures seemed small at first; the occasional plant closure as a result of early foreign competition, scattered threats to the environment from years of heavy industrial production, and economic uncertainty in communities that over relied on the old model for fiscal stability.

The flaws kept getting bigger and deeper over the next few decades heading towards the new millennium when…

BANG!

The global economy with all of its power and force hit us like a ton of bricks. Suddenly Michigan, and all that it was built upon, appeared completely mismatched with the new world around it. Big corporations were getting hammered by start-ups. Old style manufacturing was being off-loaded to southern states and developing countries, and domestic manufacturing was going super high tech. And the once proud "company man" was literally and figuratively being replaced by the wide-eyed entrepreneur. In short, old school Michigan blinked its eyes as an industrial capital of the world and woke up to find itself in the global economy's version of the Wild, Wild West.

While other parts of the country were embracing the new normal, Michigan seemed as if it was collapsing in on itself. Per capita income, once in the top ten among states, fell to 37th in 2009. The state's two largest metro regions, Detroit and Grand Rapids, fell to 37th and 45th (out of 51 metropolitan regions nationally) respectively, in the number of residents with college degrees. Our foreclosure rates and unemployment were some of the highest in the nation. I could go on, but I won't. We do too much of that in our state.

In 2005, the Michigan Municipal League, like dozens of associations, foundations and academics, stepped up its efforts and decided to take on the challenge of weeding through all of the data in an attempt to find a clear path for the state that would lead us out of our economic purgatory.

Our studies started where most others have—looking at the impact of our tax structure on business, the positive and negative effect of the state's regulatory environment on job creation, and the quality of our public schools. These issues have dominated the economic development debate in Michigan for decades and many "in the know" believe we must address these issues above all else before moving on to other avenues. But it is next to impossible to find a link between what the business-as-usual crowd deems to be friendly tax and regulatory environments in other states and associated strong economies. And, while nobody doubts that it is hugely important to have a strong public education system in place, underperforming public schools in Chicago, Washington, D.C. and other big cities didn't seem to impede their overall economic progress, at least in the short run.

So we kept looking. And what we and our partners are finding is both shocking and obvious at the same time.

"IT'S THE PLACE, STUPID!"

Let's digress for a moment to contrast the migration of one middle class American family in the 1950s to a group of upstarts in the new millennium.

Shortly after World War II when Ward Cleaver of *Leave It to Beaver,* asked June to marry him, they dreamed of getting out of the city and raising their children in one of those promising new burgs that were popping up across the country. Ward's comfortable job in middle management allowed him to trade in his transit ticket for a brand new automobile and head out of town on one of those eight lane highways that the federal government was building in all directions.

The place that they found themselves seemed idyllic. Ward and June made lots of friends with the other couples who moved to town to work in the same industry. All of the houses looked just alike. There were new indoor shopping malls, too, that would make it certain that everybody dressed alike, listened to similar music, and ate at the same restaurants. And their two sons, the studious Wally and that precocious little Beaver, would go to brand new schools built seemingly just for them. Since there wasn't much history in these new places, or at least it didn't seem to be valued much, all of the schools would predictably be named after prominent national figures regardless of their connection to the people in the area. (Author's note: for disclosure's sake, I will admit to having attended public schools named for Hoover, Holmes, and Stevenson, even though I have found no evidence that any of them ever set foot in my city.)

So, basically, they were just like everyone else that they knew. And they were happy.

Now let's fast forward to 2000. The brave, new post World War II world that attracted the Cleavers and millions like them to places like the one on Mapleton Street, appeared just as dated as the cities that they thought they had left behind a generation ago. Mirroring the new international trend, a group of young, highly educated "Friends" named Joey, Rachel, Phoebe, Monica, Ross, and Chandler took up residence in neighboring apartments in the Big Apple where they could find excitement and pursue their version of the American Dream. They toiled as an actor, a fashion consultant, a musician, a chef, a paleontologist, and an executive in the statistical analysis field. Think Richard Florida's creative class[1] types, only better looking.

This group would shun the homogenous lifestyles of their parents for a chance to make it in an urban environment that included culture, diversity (the city, not the cast), and entrepreneurial opportunities. They didn't own cars and walked everywhere, too. By choice!

So, basically, they were just like everyone else that they knew. And they were happy.

The fact that both *Leave It to Beaver* and *Friends* were mega hits in their day, speaks to their settings and how people would relate to the characters on the show. Ward and June's comfortable dwelling fit the model of what Americans preferred in the '50s and '60s, and the *Friends* setting seemed like paradise to young professionals seeking authenticity and energy in the '90s and 2000s. I question whether or not either setting would have worked if their running dates were reversed.

So why make the comparison?

For those of us interested in building fantastic contemporary places, the contrasts of these two productions offer important lessons in demography, marketing, and city building. What makes something great in one era may not hold up in another one—like Laurel & Hardy. And while we can't easily, nor should we try to, change the underlying fabric of our communities, we need to acquire a deep understanding of what will make communities more competitive now and in the future, and actively seek to push them in this direction.

BRAINS ARE BEAUTIFUL

We know that educational attainment is the biggest predictor of success for cities and metro areas today. The research is unassailable.

---

1 Florida, Richard. *The Rise of the Creative Class: And How It's Transforming Work, Leisure, Community and Everyday Life*. Basic Books, 2002.

Downtown Dexter, Michigan. Courtesy of the Michigan Municipal League

Increasing educational attainment, measured by raising the four-year college attainment rate by one percentage point in each of America's 51 largest metropolitan areas, would be associated with an increase in per capita income of $124 billion per year for the nation. And each additional percentage point improvement in aggregate adult four-year college attainment in a city is associated with a $763 increase in annual per capita income.[2]

The knowledge-based economy that we find ourselves immersed in is here to stay. The lower skill, higher wage factory jobs that defined states like Michigan and cities like Detroit have largely disappeared. Simply stated, in today's economy the places with the most brains win. And while I am pleased to report that the tired mindset that says that we can rebuild these old style economies according to a 20th century blueprint appears to be on life support, the more difficult nut to crack is breaking from the old political and governmental mindsets that dictate how important public policy decisions are made.

So if the quality of a local or regional workforce is indeed the indicator of a strong economy (as it is in places like Seattle, Boston, and Minneapolis), then we must make sure that Michigan is appropriately aligned with this new paradigm. But, where should we begin?

"We know that educational attainment is the biggest predictor of success for cities and metro areas today. The research is unassailable.[3]"

Cut Taxes?

With apologies to many of my friends who represent traditional business organizations, you guys need a new playbook. Finding a correlation between low tax states like Mississippi and high income states like Massachusetts is near impossible, although I will submit that they both start with the same letter. I loathe paying taxes as much as the next guy and advocate for squeezing more out of every dollar raised, but simply cutting taxes and expecting the growth to follow in an environment that increasingly depends on quality of place is a scheme hatched in some anti-tax Disneyland where no actual data exists.[4] Worse yet, the tax debate continues to sap energy and it keeps us from acting on what really matters economically.

---

2 CEOs for Cities Talent Dividend, CEOs for Cities, 2011.

3 CEOs for Cities Talent Dividend, CEOs for Cities, 2011.

4 New Agenda for a New Michigan, Michigan Future, Inc., 2009.

Loosen Regulations on Business?

Have you ever tried to open a business in Chicago? Or New York? Or Seattle? Not the friendliest of business environments. Yet new innovations are popping up within their borders and in numerous places just like them across the country. Responsible local and state governments must regularly update their regulatory processes in an effort to create the best environment possible. But try asking a promising young entrepreneur if she prefers her city to have a relaxed environmental policy or a commitment to support sustainability. I bet she chooses the latter. To her it is not just a fad to "be green," it is a value. And the regulatory environment plays a distant second fiddle to the quality of the place where she dwells and pursues her piece of the dream.

Bust the Unions?

Here is another 20th century remedy to a 21st century problem. While I have a laundry list of points where I think organized labor is missing the boat, turning $20-an-hour jobs with benefits into $10-an-hour jobs without them, isn't a healthy and sustainable growth strategy unless you're Malaysia. Check the statistics.

Attract and Retain Talented People?

BINGO.

And how do we do that, you ask? It's simple. OK, maybe it's not so simple. We achieve this through building and sustaining high quality places in our state.

CREATING QUALITY PLACES TO LIVE, WORK, LEARN AND PLAY

So what does it mean for community builders and government officials? It means that we need to forget much of what we learned in the last half of the 20th century and begin implementing new strategies and systems for everything from business attraction programs to service delivery methods. How soon and effectively a community is able to make these transitions will be directly related to their ultimate success and sustainability. At the League, we have broken all of it down into the following Eight Assets that are now part of our Center for 21st Century Communities.

Physical Design & Walkability

Communities have been designed to shuffle people between work and home, however, market analysis continues to show that today's young professionals, baby boomers, and empty nesters want to live in neighborhoods with walkable downtowns, access to cultural, social, and entertainment opportunities, and a variety of transportation options.

Green Initiatives

Green initiatives are critical for any community intending to be viable in today's economy. The way we use energy and natural resources impacts our quality of life and our financial bottom line. Potential to grow green industries, implement sustainable practices, and get on the cutting edge of current trends exists right here in Michigan.

Cultural Economic Development

Arts and culture are essential components of a thriving, knowledge-based economy. A healthy creative sector attracts and retains residents and businesses, and produces economic benefits including jobs, a stronger tax base, downtown and neighborhood revitalization, and tourism.

Entrepreneurship

Growing knowledge-based jobs in ones and twos creates sustainable economies in the 21st century. Strategies that solely focus on seeking out large manufacturers and big box retailers overlook the positive impact that entrepreneurs and small businesses have on local communities.

Multiculturalism

Creating and sustaining a genuine commitment to diversity and multiculturalism in Michigan's

ANN ARBOR

Historic Montage. Artists: Rob Zell-Breier & Bruce Loeschen

MICHIGAN

Courtesy of www.communitycreations.com

communities is vital to attracting key demographics and global businesses. Today's fluid, mobile, and, most importantly, global workforce is seeking out "the right kind of place" that embraces people of all religions, ethnicities, national origins, and races.

Messaging & Technology

Next generation internet and communication technologies, known as Web 2.0, are connecting people and allowing them to share information in the virtual world in unprecedented ways. Social networking applications like Twitter, Facebook, MySpace, and YouTube, as well as communication platforms like blogs and Wikis, are not just for kids anymore.

Transit

Developing effective public transit options in Michigan is a necessary tool for attracting and retaining residents, workers, and businesses. Research shows that people across the nation are choosing communities that offer various modes of transportation, easy access to the places they live, work, and play, and allow them to travel without having to rely on a car. In particular, systems like streetcars and light rail have been credited with sparking new commercial and residential development.

Education

Educational institutions, pre-kindergarten through college, play a central role in growing a knowledge-based economy and encouraging a more engaged citizenry. As anchor institutions, colleges and universities bring opportunities for entertainment, arts and culture, healthcare, and recreation, and serve as engines of economic development.

A NEW PHILOSOPHY

How individual neighborhoods, communities, regions, and states attempt to deal with these issues is only limited by their willingness to pioneer solutions for implementation. Revolutionary change is clearly needed in many traditional governmental service delivery areas. The good news is that the combination of civic engagement and innovative applied technologies are making revolution easier. The League, for example, is working in certain communities in Michigan to create real sustainability in non-profit organizations and neighborhood groups so that they can provide formal assistance to local governments in areas ranging from nuisance abatement ("deputizing" neighborhood groups to identify potential enforcement issues) to food services (eliminating endless red tape for local growers; and food carts, too!) and even in the public safety arena (public/private partnerships). There are countless other groups that are doing similar work in communities around the world in areas like economic development, housing, and arts & culture.

The products of enlightened civic engagement and the continued evolution of these "micro governance" models is a win-win situation for those involved. The work helps to alleviate financial burdens of struggling governmental agencies while providing new systems and services that are more in keeping with what will be needed to make these places economically competitive in 2011 and beyond.

Swapping entrenched sacred cows for innovative strategies, creating new delivery methods for delivering traditional government services, and fostering effective community engagement should be the measuring stick for which we all live by.

DANIEL GILMARTIN serves as the executive director and CEO of the Michigan Municipal League, the state's association of communities formed in 1899. He directs the League's programming, policy development, and member services. Gilmartin previously served as the League's deputy director, and as the organization's lead lobbyist in Lansing and in Washington. Through his work on behalf of municipalities, Gilmartin is recognized as a statewide leader in the fields of urban revitalization, local government reform, and transportation policy. Recognizing that communities are at the core of the economic turnaround of Michigan, he is a passionate leader for making sure we create vibrant, creative communities for the future, not the past.

In 2010, Gilmartin added radio talk show host to his resume as host of The Prosperity Agenda on News/Talk 760 WJR, which is Michigan's highest-rated talk station that can be heard throughout the Midwest and parts of Canada. The show focuses on the critical importance that strong and vibrant communities must play if Michigan is to improve its economic outlook in the 21st century economy.

Downtown Northville, Michigan. Courtesy of the Michigan Municipal League

the path to prosperity

LOU GLAZER

MICHIGAN PER CAPITA

2000
ranked 18th

2009
ranked 37th

For most of the last century Michigan was one of the most prosperous places on the planet. No more! What happened? What made us prosperous for nearly 100 years—an extraordinarily long run—was the abundance of good-paying, low-education attainment jobs, primarily in manufacturing. In a flattening world driven by technology and globalization, those jobs are gone.

Several years ago, we predicted that Michigan's per capita income would fall to the mid 30s because it is increasingly correlated with a state's ranking in college attainment. Michigan is 36th in the proportion of adults with a four-year degree. We first made the prediction when the state was still in the mid 20s in per capita income.

Our prediction quickly turned out to be right. In 2009, we fell to 37th. We are now almost 19 percent below the national average, by far our worst since the feds started keeping statistics in 1929. In 2000, we were 18th in per capita income, about 4 percent below the national average. In nine years, 19 states passed us, and compared to the country we are 15 percent poorer. An unprecedented collapse!

When we made our prediction, hardly anyone believed us. In essence they asked, "What does college attainment have to do with income?" They believed that since it didn't matter in the 20th century, when we were one of the most prosperous places on the planet, no way is it predictive now. They hadn't learned the lesson then—and most still haven't—that what made us prosperous in the past won't in the future. There is no turning the clock back to the mass middle class Michigan invented, which was anchored by high wage, low-education attainment jobs.

The American economy is going through a profound structural transformation from an industrial-based to a knowledge-based economy.

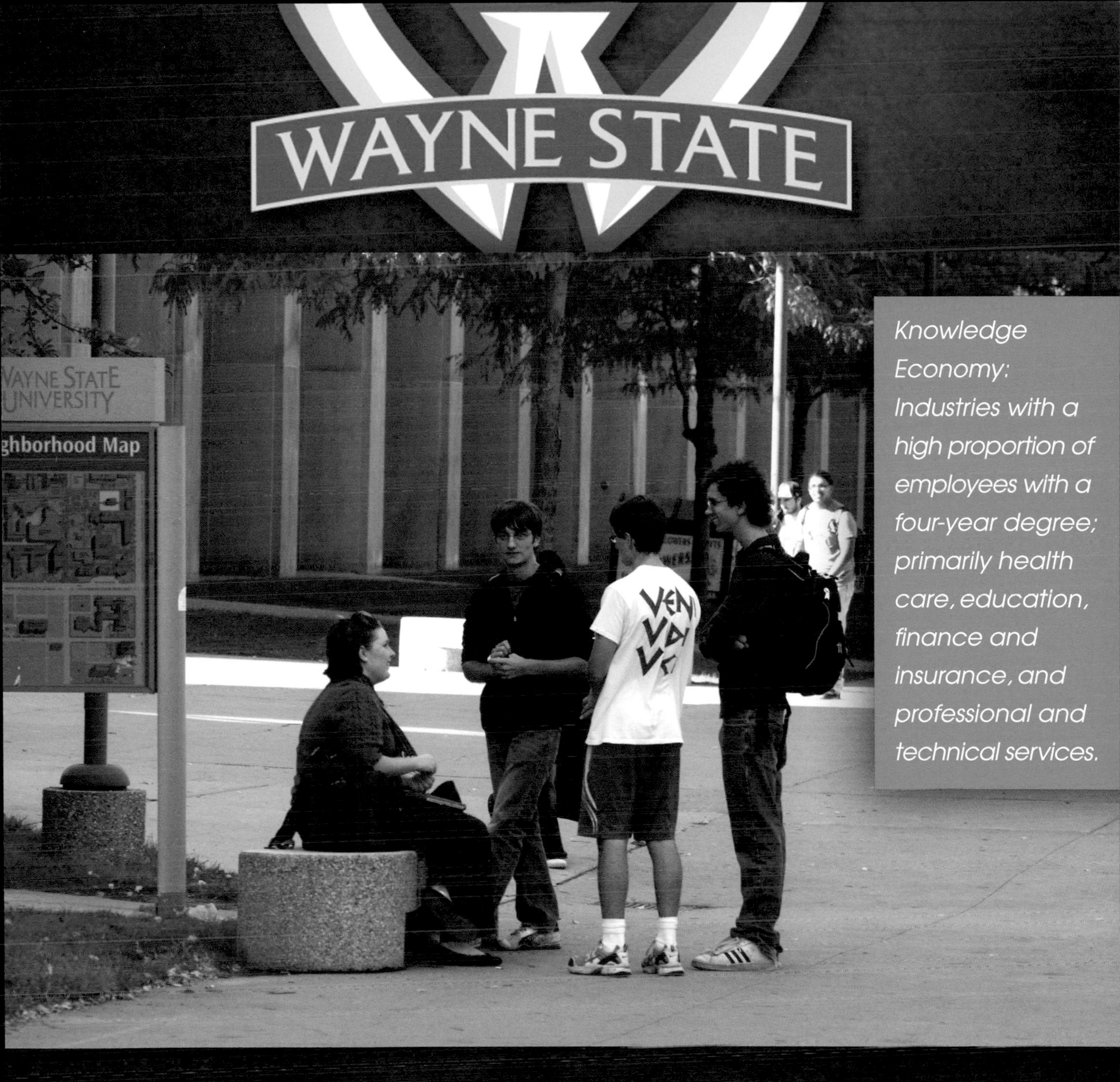

Knowledge Economy: Industries with a high proportion of employees with a four-year degree; primarily health care, education, finance and insurance, and professional and technical services.

The Wayne State Campus, Detroit, Michigan. Courtesy of the Michigan Municipal League

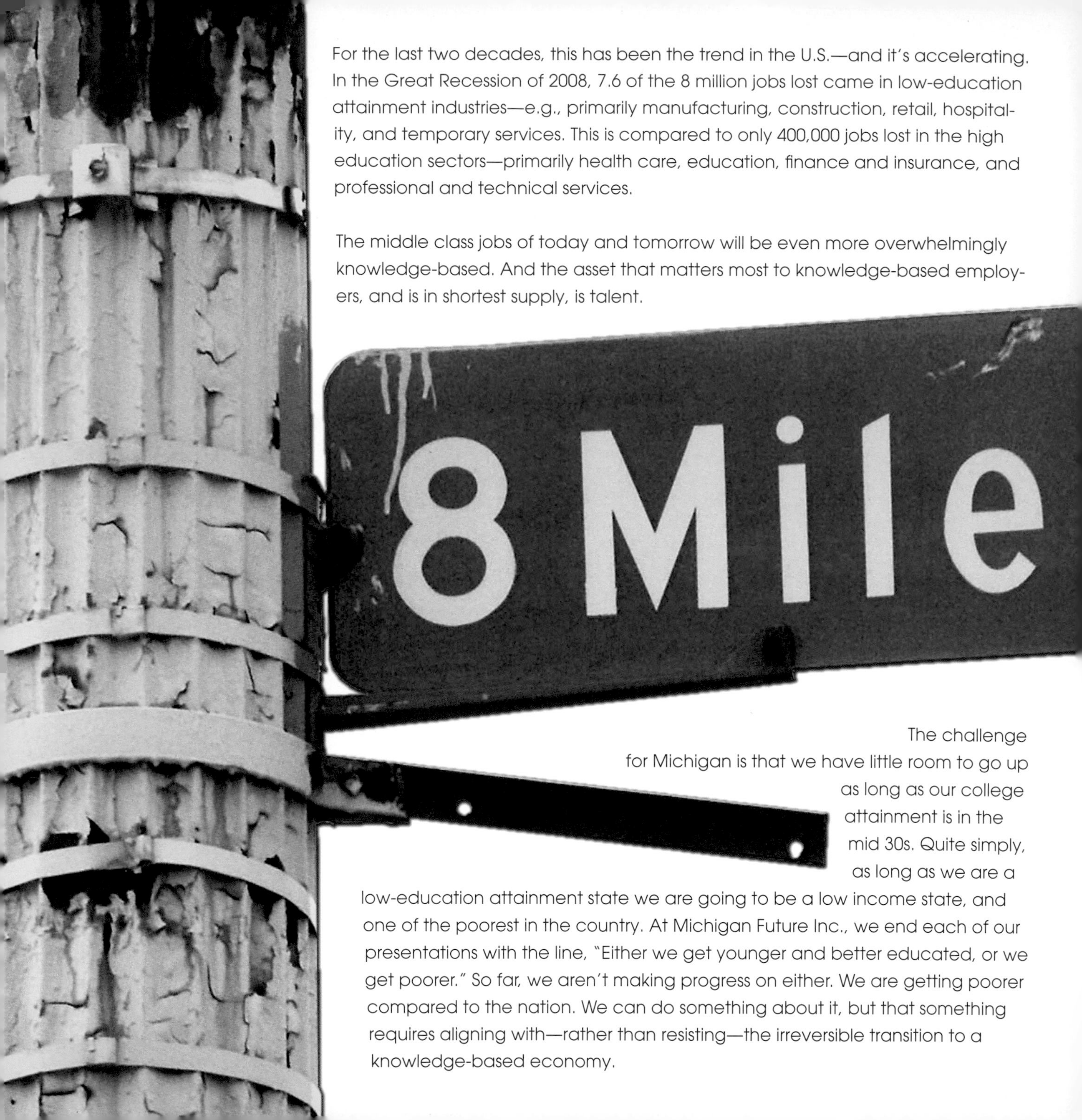

For the last two decades, this has been the trend in the U.S.—and it's accelerating. In the Great Recession of 2008, 7.6 of the 8 million jobs lost came in low-education attainment industries—e.g., primarily manufacturing, construction, retail, hospitality, and temporary services. This is compared to only 400,000 jobs lost in the high education sectors—primarily health care, education, finance and insurance, and professional and technical services.

The middle class jobs of today and tomorrow will be even more overwhelmingly knowledge-based. And the asset that matters most to knowledge-based employers, and is in shortest supply, is talent.

The challenge for Michigan is that we have little room to go up as long as our college attainment is in the mid 30s. Quite simply, as long as we are a low-education attainment state we are going to be a low income state, and one of the poorest in the country. At Michigan Future Inc., we end each of our presentations with the line, "Either we get younger and better educated, or we get poorer." So far, we aren't making progress on either. We are getting poorer compared to the nation. We can do something about it, but that something requires aligning with—rather than resisting—the irreversible transition to a knowledge-based economy.

MICHIGAN 3.0

If 2011 is to be a start of a long-term Michigan economic recovery, it will be because we get on the path to the Michigan 3.0 for which Governor Snyder campaigned. The challenge is that most of the Legislature that was elected with him campaigned on restoring Michigan 2.0.

The decision we make on which direction we head in will go a long way towards defining our economic future. Move towards Michigan 3.0, and we can once again be one of the most prosperous places on the planet. Stay as Michigan 2.0, and we will continue to lag behind the rest of the nation.

Unfortunately, what appears to be the preeminent vision of a successful future Michigan is really a "turn the clock back" economy still anchored by factories, farms, and tourism. It won't work!

The hard truths Michiganians need to confront:

1. Michigan's prosperity in the last century was built primarily on good paying, low-education attainment jobs. Many of those jobs are gone forever.

2. The auto industry—although still important—will never again be the major engine of prosperity in Michigan. It will be substantially smaller, employ far fewer, and will pay its workers less with fewer benefits.

2011 will almost certainly be, for the first time in more than a decade, a year of net job growth in Michigan. The chief reason for those gains is once again the domestic auto industry, the same engine that has driven Michigan for the past century. But today it is a much weaker engine. No one expects it to be a major growth engine for the state once it's back up, after its near demise the last two years.

The decline in autos is part of an irreversible new reality that manufacturing—work done in factories—is no longer a sustainable source of high-paid jobs, nor is it a source of future job growth. Manufacturing makes up less than 10 percent of the American workforce today and continues to decline.

3. The other industries that are widely believed to be drivers of the Michigan economy—farming and tourism—are also not a source of many good-paying jobs. Less than 2 percent of Michiganians work on a farm and, on average, it is not a high-paying industry. Tourism, although a likely source of job growth, is also a low-wage industry.

SOME TOUGH QUESTIONS

The bottom line is if the Michigan economy of the future is built on a base of factories, farms, and tourism, then we will be a low-prosperity state. So if the economy of the past—Michigan 1.0 and 2.0—isn't the answer, what is? Our answer is high prosperity—a Michigan with a multitude of good-paying jobs, a broad middle class, and a realistic chance for families to realize the American Dream. High prosperity is different from the most-often-used measure for economic success—low unemployment. There are many areas across the country with low unemployment but also with low incomes. That isn't success to us.

The term Millennials is referred to as the group of young people between the ages of 24 to 35.

In developing our strategy for a high prosperity Michigan, we started with the question, "What really matters as we work to position Michigan and its regions for success in a knowledge-based, global economy?" We tried to learn what distinguished the most prosperous states from us. We read a lot, collected data, and talked extensively with thought leaders in and outside of Michigan.

Our starting point was this premise: "In a world where technology and globalization are driving fundamental structural change in the U.S. economy, Michigan's slower job growth has not been caused by the loss of manufacturing jobs. The entire country is losing work done in factories. Michigan is lagging the nation because of our slow growth in the dynamic, high wage sectors of the knowledge economy."

We then asked ourselves, "What are the characteristics of high prosperity, knowledge-based state economies?" First, we concluded that state economies can best be understood not as political jurisdictions, but as the sum of their regional economies. Second, what distinguishes successful metro regions from Michigan regions are significantly higher concentrations of knowledge-based industries and the proportion of adults with post-secondary, undergraduate, and advanced degrees of study. Finally, prosperous regions generally are anchored by vital core cities that attract knowledge-based workers.

Through the lens of these high prosperity characteristics, think about our challenges in Michigan where too often Detroit vs outstate regions or cities vs townships trump regional economic strategies; where what we export to the rest of the world even today remains highly dependent on auto-related manufacturing that will continue to adjust to global economics and a smaller market share; where race, politics, and demographic trends have resulted in educational decline and economic and social disinvestment in most Michigan core cities. These challenges are not a Detroit-only problem.

In 2008, of the 55 U.S. metro areas with populations of 1 million or more, Detroit ranked 33rd in knowledge-based industries concentration, 36th in per capita income, and 37th in college attainment. Metro Grand Rapids lagged even more, ranking 54th in knowledge-based industries concentration, 53rd in per capita income, and 45th in college attainment.

And when your big metros struggle, so does your state. The pattern across the country is clear. Nearly all high prosperity states have big metropolitan areas with even higher per capita income. So it is not a surprise that in 2009, Michigan's per capita income fell again to 37th.

What matters most in turning around these measures and better positioning Michigan regions for success in a knowledge-driven, global economy? Our conclusion is talent. Rich Karlgaard, publisher of *Forbes* magazine, sums it up, saying, "Best place to make a future *Forbes* 400 fortune? Start with this proposition: the most valuable natural resource of the 21st century is brains. Smart people tend to be mobile. Watch where they go! Because wherever they go, robust economic activity will follow." In a flat world, where work can be done anywhere on the planet, economic development priority #1 is to prepare, retain, and attract talent.

We also concluded that this focus on talent requires a rethinking of our strategy to grow Michigan's economy. There are no quick fixes. Michigan's economy is going to continue to lag for the foreseeable future. But there is a path back to high prosperity—to Michigan 3.0.

SIX PRIORITIES IN BECOMING A HIGH-PROSPERITY STATE

Our rethinking resulted in six priorities we believe will expand Michigan's talent base and, therefore, the vitality of our regions.

1. Build a Michigan culture aligned with the flat world. More important than legislative policy changes are the attitudes and beliefs of Michigan families about how to get ahead in a world of constant change. That the old Michigan economy worked so well for so many of us is now a barrier to our future success.

In an age where economic growth is driven by knowledge and innovation, the most prosperous regions are those that highly value learning, an entrepreneurial spirit, and being welcoming to all. The evidence is that Michigan is having trouble with all three. One measure of learning is our ranking of 37th of 50 states in the percentage of adults with a four-year degree. Over the past 15 years, Michigan has been one of the leading exporters of college-educated young adults. The just-completed U.S. Census tells us that 21 to 34 year olds make up 17.6 percent of our state's population compared to 19.1 percent nationally—that we are becoming a less populated, older state. Survey research also indicates that too many parents still do not believe there is an essential link between post-secondary education and their children's job prospects in today's economy.

The entrepreneurial spirit that launched great automobiles, cereal, furniture, pharmaceutical, and chemical enterprises in Michigan, over time, has been replaced by a mindset that employment is less about risk taking and more about an entitlement to a long-term, well-paying job.

Projections are that by mid-century, American society will have become an even richer tapestry of race, ethnicity and religion. With white Americans realizing minority status, we are one of the nation's most racially segregated states, and there is mounting evidence of increased hostility towards immigrants and homosexuals. In a world where talent is both increasingly mobile and coming from every group, the places that are welcoming to all will do best.

We cannot legislate a change in culture, but we must address more openly these cultural barriers to the reinvention of Michigan's economy, and work intentionally to become more welcoming.

2. New leadership. Transforming Michigan's culture will occur more rapidly if we invite into our state regional leadership, those representing the change we are trying to achieve—the young, well-educated, and entrepreneurial. Representative of the need for new leadership, is a 2010 *Crain's Detroit Business* list of the 25 most connected leaders in metro Detroit. None were associated with new economy businesses, and all but two were in their 50s or older.

We need the inclusion of new and younger leadership in quality of life and economic development initiatives, particularly those who are working in knowledge-based enterprises or groups that compete nationally and internationally for talent. Maybe most importantly, we need leaders willing to speak the hard truth to Michigan; nothing can be done to get their old jobs back, and the path to prosperity requires all of us to change.

3. Align pre K-12 with a knowledge-driven economy. As a nation, we have expended so much effort to improve schools over the past decade. But no clear set of reforms with a high probability of success has emerged. Yet if we are ever going to narrow the gap between rich and poor, between educated and uneducated families, we must insist on accessible, quality K-12 schools throughout our regions.

In fact, learning begins at birth. The scientific evidence is clear that most of a person's brain development occurs in the first four years of life, and that those who experience nurturing and learning during infancy will be better prepared to succeed in school. When looking at competition between regions, those metro areas that are funding expansive pre-K learning programs, especially for disadvantaged children, will likely have the most solid learning foundations necessary to prepare talent in the years ahead.

As for K-12 success, we found no evidence of a strong correlation between the amount of spending on schools and stronger economies or better student achievement. It's also clear that the form of school governance is no magic bullet. Despite claims by advocates on all sides, the evidence is that in each system—district, public charter, parochial, and independent—there are not enough quality schools.

There are no shortcuts. We are going to have to do the hard work to develop quality teaching and learning from birth to retirement. We need to develop educators—from classroom teachers to superintendents to college presidents—

who are thoroughly grounded in the realities of the flat world in which we live. And we need to give them the ability to experiment and innovate, so they can prepare all students for the flat world and instill in children a love of learning and the ability to be curious, adaptable lifelong learners. And because children are wired differently for learning, we must make available more school and learning path choices for students.

4. Invest in higher education, first and foremost. This is what Bill Gates recently told the National Conference of State Legislatures: "Take the two big leading industries…biology and medicine, that's one, and computer technology, that's two. The job creation and the success for those industries have been overwhelmingly in the locations where there is a great university. There's an almost perfect correlation between the number of jobs in a region and the strength of universities."

17.6%

of the population in Michigan is aged

21-34

vs.

19.1%

nationally

As we assessed the assets Michigan presently has to prepare, retain, and attract home-grown, national and international talent, our higher education system—both universities and community colleges—was at the top of our list. We believe the single most important step policy makers can take for the future economic success of Michigan is to ensure the long-term vitality and agility of our higher education system.

Unfortunately, after decades of building a world-class system, more recently the state has been underinvesting in our universities and community colleges. Over the past ten years, state funding for higher education has been cut by 27 percent, which reflects the fact that higher education has been a less important state priority than prisons and tax cuts.

We recommend a restoration of our commitment to higher education institutions, but in a manner that would bring more accountability, accessibility, and talent to the system. We propose providing state funding directly to students, no matter where they come from—in or outside of Michigan—rather than funding the institutions themselves. What will matter most to Michigan's economic future is not where students grow up, but where they choose to live and work after college. So our preference would be to provide at least some of the funding, per student, in the form of loans that would become grants for those who stayed and worked in Michigan for at least three to five years after college.

Of particular importance is support for our major research universities. They are arguably the most important assets Michigan has in building Michigan 3.0. Today, Michigan universities annually bring in more than $1.5 billion of federal research dollars and employ thousands of knowledge workers. In addition, our research universities are major attractors of talent from around the world. Although there are no guarantees, places where new knowledge is being created have a big edge—that is where new technologies are commercialized. So we have proposed a 20 percent state match for federal research funds.

5. Both economic opportunity and quality of place are essential ingredients in retaining and attracting mobile talent. They both matter. Mobile talent will not stay in Michigan if job opportunities are not available.

To attract businesses with high growth potential, our report recommends a state business tax structure with a broad base and low rate. While we cannot unilaterally stop providing special tax breaks or incentives to compete against other states for new investment, we support restricting those breaks to export-based businesses only. Second, state and local regulations should be minimized and streamlined to encourage competition and innovation.

Finally, state government should not concentrate all of its economic development efforts on trying to choose industries of the future in which to invest. Our report concludes that a better idea than overly prescriptive state investments is to support basic research at our universities and non-profit research institutions and push them to drive commercialization efforts.

6. Build regions that are attractive places to live. Governor Snyder's assessment in his ten-point plan that "many of Michigan's youth are looking for an appealing metropolitan community—and many are moving out of state to find it" is right. His list of quality of place attributes that are needed to compete for mobile young talent include: safe/walkable urban neighborhoods with vibrant third places (locations for social opportunities); transit; parks/outdoor recreation; and the arts.

The millennials, more than any previous generation, are concentrating in big metropolitan areas anchored by vibrant central cities. For Michigan to prosper, its central cities, particularly Detroit, must be places where young mobile talent wants to live and work.

This requires public investment in housing, attractive public gathering places, the arts, and the commercial businesses that follow in our core cities. It is also why we need renewed federal and state urban revenue sharing, and housing and transit policies designed to create more livable, sustainable, urban communities.

A corollary to the six priorities is the role of taxes and a public investment strategy. We cannot legislate the needed change from an entitlement culture to a learning, entrepreneurial, welcoming culture, nor can we simply tax cut our path to prosperity.

Our analysis of extensive tax and economic data found that the most successful states are not characterized by low taxes. If anything, they tend to be more high tax states than low. On the other hand, states with the lowest taxes tend to have lower per capita incomes, lower concentrations in knowledge-based enterprises, and lower proportions of adults with four-year degrees or more. Again, I quote Bill Gates in his presentation to state legislators, "The industries that I think about the most, information technology and biological industries…are more sensitive to the quality of talent in a location than they are to the tax policies."

We all would like Mississippi's taxes and Minnesota's economy, but there is no state in the nation that has both. Michigan's last decade was not caused by high taxes, high spending, or irresponsible elected officials unwilling to make tough decisions. When it comes to state budgets, we actually did better than most. The reality is that for the past decade Michigan has lowered taxes and spending, which have been accompanied by slower economic growth here than in the rest of the nation.

We had a lost decade primarily because our preeminent industry—the Detroit Three—collapsed. We did not have an alternative engine to offset its collapse. The sooner we learn the lesson that copying low tax and spending states has little or nothing to do with building that alternative engine, which is the key to rebuilding the Michigan economy, the better.

We are not suggesting our tax burden should be uncompetitive with other states. But tax policy should not undermine our ability to invest in the human and physical infrastructure necessary for economic growth investments like higher education, early childhood learning, quality of life amenities, transportation and transit, and vital urban centers. We know moving to Michigan 3.0 is scary and difficult. But the payoff from success is huge. At the turn of the last century, we were America's Silicon Valley.

Through pure innovation, Michigan created the 20th century's broad middle class. And we can do it again—but only if we embrace what's next, rather than hanging on to what once was.

The author wishes to thank former state House Speaker Paul Hillegonds for many of his thoughts and ideas that he presented at "The Next 50 Years in Michigan" at the Grand Valley State University Distinguished Lecture Series, February 16, 2011.

Lou Glazer is president and co-founder of Michigan Future, Inc. (MFI), a non-partisan, non-profit organization. Michigan Future's mission is to be a source of new ideas on how Michigan can succeed as a world-class community in a knowledge-driven economy. Its work is funded by Michigan foundations.

Its two latest reports are: "Michigan's Transition to a Knowledge-Based Economy," which provides a progress report on how well Michigan is positioned to succeed in a flattening world. And "Young Talent in the Great Lakes," an analysis of Michigan's success in retaining and attracting college-educated millennials. Prior to joining MFI, Glazer served as deputy director of the Michigan Department of Commerce during the Blanchard administration. He received his bachelor's and master's degrees from the University of Michigan.

---

quality of place: the talent driver

CAROL COLETTA

Let me tell you a story about my earliest experience with place.

I grew up in a small, two-bedroom fieldstone house in Memphis, Tennessee. It was the type of neighborhood where the children barged into the house next door without knocking. I could walk around the corner to the grocery store, the drug store, the library, and the movie theatre. Going a bit farther and I could walk to school.

It was, you could say, "intimate."

When I turned 12, I realized that only a block away from home I could take the 13 Lauderdale bus to downtown Memphis—without adult supervision. There, I would discover a wide new world—glamorous department stores, art, live music, new friends from different neighborhoods, and strange people doing strange things. I didn't know it then, but I was raised in the perfect place. It was what we now label a "10-minute neighborhood" connected to the city's major employment and cultural center by transit.

Back then, the population of Memphis was 500,000—and it was so vibrant. Every place was pulsing, including downtown. We were all neighbors, living in 128 square miles. There were almost 4,000 of us per square mile.

Forty years later, the population of Memphis is 650,000—and it feels empty. The city pursued a multiple centers concept when, in truth, the city could support only a single robust center. Memphians—yes, that's what they're called—are now spread over almost three times the number of square miles, and density is now 2,000 fewer people per square mile. People hardly feel like neighbors, they certainly don't act like neighbors, and they share few public experiences.

That, in one small story, is as good of an explanation of the difference between places that work and places that don't as you're going to get from me.

Well-made cities, in fact, have certain natural advantages. We call that effect "The City Advantage."

Hernando de Soto Bridge, Memphis, Tennessee. Courtesy of Wikipedia

THE DESIGNED CITIES

Well-made cities—cities that are compact and diverse, have mixed-uses, and where transportation choices are easy and plentiful—naturally have a greater variety of choices. They are more convenient, with more choices close at hand. They offer more opportunity in the form of access to education and jobs. And they are places of discovery where you can find people, things, and experiences you didn't even know you wanted.

It turns out that wages, productivity, and entrepreneurship rise with density. Intellectual spillovers that drive innovation and employment drop off dramatically as firms and people move more than a mile apart. The bigger the city, the more the average citizen owns, produces, and consumes—whether they be goods, resources, or ideas.

As Edward Glaeser, professor of economics at Harvard University says, density doesn't just make cities more productive; it makes them more fun.

But in too many of our cities, we've destroyed these natural advantages by doing what Memphis did. We spread too few people over too much land. We make it impossible to serve people efficiently with transit. We move jobs too far away from the people who need them. We dissipate any vitality the core city might have. We discourage walking and biking. We make traffic congestion inevitable and increasing carbon emissions a certainty. We turn parents into chauffeurs and seniors into prisoners in their own homes.

What were we thinking?

Well, clearly, we weren't.

And in too many places, we still aren't.

Chicago, where I now live, has taken a decidedly different path: a strengthened city core animated 24/7 by a revitalized theatre district and lots of new and converted housing, all served by a robust transit system; a sophisticated climate action plan driven by a strong mayor; and, of course, Millennium Park. This jewel of a green roof, converted from a huge parking eyesore, completely changed the real estate dynamics in the Chicago Loop, giving new value to C-class office buildings, sparking retail and restaurant activity on every approach to the park, and creating what I predict will become the city's most enduring great place.

Crown Fountain in Millennium Park, Chicago, Illinois. Courtesy of Serge Melki

MYTH VS REALITY

None of this has been easy. Because in America, sadly, we still imagine ourselves as some bucolic nation with mom, dad, and 2.3 children living behind the white picket fence—family life right out of a 1950s sitcom.

The reality of America is very different. The U.S. is, in fact, an urban nation with 80 percent of us living and working in metro America. Seventy-five to 90 percent of the nation's economic assets and drivers are in metro areas. The contribution cities make to the metro output is disproportionate—much greater than their population and certainly their space. In fact, a third of all Americans live in just 16 cities.

When you look at the facts, it's hard to argue that there is any path to America's success other than the path that runs right through successful cities.

But we're not yet quite ready to admit it. Isn't it odd that when you attach the word "urban" to almost anything, it seems worse? Urban poverty is worse than poverty. Urban crime is worse than crime. And that really gets in the way of understanding that the future of the nation—the future of the planet—depends on the success of cities.

The good news is that many of the factors that underlie how we live and the choices we make are changing in ways that favor cities. That is very good for placemakers.

Consider the changes in demographics.

Today, less than 25 percent of households are considered "traditional" with mom, dad, and kids living under the same roof. Americans are delaying marriage and childbearing, and the more educated they are, the later they marry. When they do marry, both partners are more likely to work. And many, of course, are never marrying.

More singles, more power couples, fewer families with children, delayed marriage, and delayed childbearing become sort of the perfect demographic for city living. I, however, raised three children in the heart of downtown and am convinced it was the best place for child-rearing for working moms—less chauffeuring, more villagers to raise the child, more family time together in the neighborhood, gradual growth into independence instead of the sudden leap at age 16 resulting from car dependence. So I think families belong there, too.

Idealistic 1950s family. Courtesy of Wikipedia

DRAMATIC ECONOMIC SHIFTS

Of course, we are all too familiar with the dramatic economic shifts.
Not too long ago, bigger was always better. In the U.S., we believed that real estate values would always go up, and gas would always be cheap. Conventional wisdom said that people would move anywhere for a job, labor would be equally plentiful across cities, and the competition among cities was regional.

WalkScores

A tool to evaluate your walkability and transit in your community.

Go to ***www.walkscore.com***

Well, things have changed. The bets on rising real estate values are all off. People now say they value the community as much as the house because community gets you through the tough times. We all need a network.

The increasing price of gas has made driving to qualify for a mortgage a losing proposition. That is why foreclosures were more likely to occur farthest from the city center and home buyers are willing to pay more for homes with better than average WalkScores, which measure how many everyday destinations are nearby. The higher prices for homes with higher WalkScores also likely reflect a desire for more convenience in our time-starved lives. We're also seeing nascent signs of shifts in values in the U.S.

CARS BECOMING LESS IMPORTANT

The car is becoming less relevant to a growing number of people under age 30. In 1978, nearly half of 16-year-olds and three-quarters of 17-year-olds in the U.S. had their driver's licenses. By 2008, only 31 percent of 16-year-olds and 49 percent of 17-year-olds had licenses, and the decline has accelerated rapidly since 1998. And it's not just new drivers who are driving less. The share of automobile miles driven by people ages 21 to 30 in the U.S. fell to 13.7 percent in 2009, from 18.3 percent in 2001, and 20.8 percent in 1995.

While interest in cars has sharply declined among young Americans, interest in cycling is increasing. Just look at New York. The number of cyclists in New York City increased a whopping 28 percent in the past year. Two hundred thirty-six thousand New Yorkers are riding bikes every day, and 51,000 New Yorkers started biking in the last year alone. One out of every 24 vehicles in motion on New York City streets is a bike. New Yorkers travel 1.8 million miles by bike every day, and cycling is New York City's fastest-growing mode of transportation. Consider, too, the sudden interest in local food. Look at the growth in farmers markets. After growing steadily since 1994, the number of farmers markets took a big leap last year—increasing 16 percent in just one year! Think about it; it takes a lot of customers to find the ones interested in a particular farmers market delicacies. In other words, it takes what cities uniquely offer.

Automotive miles driven by ages 21-30,

13.7%

vs.

20.8%

in 1995 and

18.3%

in 2001.

Bicycling in New York City on a designated bike lane. Courtesy of www.pedbikeimages.org - Laura Sandt

Something's happening here—less driving, more cycling, demands for more local food. These are all trends emerging in cities that we would hardly have predicted just a few years ago, but as they grow, they will only make city life more appealing.

One more important trend: 25-34 year-olds are choosing to live closer to the Central Business District (CBD). In 1980, young adults were 10 percent more likely than other Americans to live within a three-mile radius of the CBD. By 1990, that percentage had increased to 12 percent. But by 2000, it had increased to 33 percent. As my colleague economist Joe Cortright likes to remind me, every city has nice suburbs, but not every city has a vibrant central city and strong close-in neighborhoods. That's a key difference among cities.

Further, thanks to the Knight Foundation and The Knight Soul of Community Poll by Gallup, we now know that the factors driving attachment to community are also changing. The top three factors now are social offerings, openness, and aesthetics.

TECHNOLOGY IS "DRIVING" CHANGE

Another shift in trends is our changing relationship to the community supported by technology.
Technology is affecting the way we use cities.

Who said distance is dead? No one predicted it, but technology is driving more face-to-face interactions, and the knowledge economy makes those interactions more valuable.

Oddly enough, technology is also making driving less desirable. Almost everything about digital media and technology makes cars less desirable or useful and makes public transportation a lot more relevant. Texting while driving is dangerous and increasingly illegal, as is watching mobile TV or working on your laptop. But you can do it on the train while someone else is driving. But when people do want to drive, they are increasingly turning to ZipCar, a car sharing service. Why own a car when you can share one? In fact, why own anything when you can rent it or borrow it, and technology can help you find it nearby? People now share vacuum cleaners, and purses—you name it. Suffused with technology, compact cities are the key to what some have called a "post-ownership prosperity."

Technology is making it possible for people to organize their own improvement initiatives—their own service provision—instead of waiting for the government to act. It has delivered an unexpected advantage to mid-size cities, allowing niche activities to find their audience via social media, and it has probably fueled the taxpayer revolt. Technology is driving a political environment where efficiency will matter. Again, all of these factors point to the growing appeal of city living that is new and improved, enabled, and even driven by technology.

Posters promoting Zip Cars, an alternative to car ownership. Courtesy of Mark Respicio

SUCCESS MEASURED BY COLLEGE GRADUATES

One final trend is the most important of all: the demography and the geography of the economy are growing lumpier. Richard Florida, author of the *Rise of the Creative Class,* called it "spiky." Even as late as August, 2010, those with four-year degrees in the U.S. had an unemployment rate of 4.6 percent, while those with only some college had an 8.7 percent unemployment rate. With a college degree in America, your average annual earnings are $59,280. With only some college, you average $21,000 less. In other words, your economic status is very much determined by your education status.

That's the story for individuals. But look at the same facts through the lens of place. It turns out that 58 percent of any city's success, when success is measured by per capita income, is predicted by the percentage of college graduates in its population.

Now layer on where talent is choosing to locate, and the implications become even more dramatic. If you look at the changes that have occurred since 1990 in where Americans with a college degree live, it's breathtaking to see how the geography of talent is morphing. People with degrees are concentrating in fewer and fewer places—leaving a lot of places wondering what they will do about the loss of talent.

Let me be clear; there are a lot more cities losing talent than gaining talent.

Keep Talent by Developing Quality of Place

So what's a city to do? A lot of urban leaders ask me that. I tell them that the engine for success in cities is talent. But developing talent is one of the most expensive things a city does. So if you spend the money to develop talent, you want to be prepared to hang on to it. How do you hang on to talent? By providing two things: quality of opportunity and quality of place.

Remember those three factors from the "Knight Soul of the Community Poll" by Gallup that create community attachment—social offerings, openness, and aesthetics?

***Social offerings* –** This flows naturally from having quality of place that puts people together in compact, vibrant settings, and is supported with a great public realm that acts as a magnet for people.

***Openness* –** That's all about quality of opportunity.

***Aesthetics* –** That's all about quality of place.

Transit options attract young talent. The North/Clybourn Train Station, Chicago, Illinois. Courtesy of Nicole Lown

As much as I believe that talent is the primary driver of city success, I believe quality of place is a deep driver of talent and where it settles. You can't separate the two. Talent and quality of place go hand in hand.

Making great places is not something you do after you've done everything else. It's not something you do only when budget times are good. In fact, I would flip that notion and assert that if budget times are going to be good, then you have to invest in quality places.

CEOs for Cities is working hard to bring this proposition to priority with urban leaders and challenging them to do more than only build an iconic place, a single light rail line, transit-oriented development, one great park, or some green buildings. All of these are worthy, but we ought to have bigger ambitions for the places we make.

We have to re-learn that context matters. I'm always surprised by some cities—the ones that won't make the tough decision to contain sprawl, but believe that a light rail line will be a game changer; or by cities that employ the "starchitect" to design the iconic museum or performing arts center, but won't invest in the arts and culture that go inside the iconic structure; or cities that invest in green buildings without considering how, and how far, people will travel to get to them.

I'll tell you a story. In the U.S., we recently celebrated the world's first certified "living buildings." So we checked the WalkScore for each of these "living buildings."

The first, in Rhinebeck, New York, had a WalkScore of 11 out of 100 points; 88% of the U.S. population lives in places with a higher WalkScore.

The second, in Tyson, Missouri, is located in a forest reserve. It's about two miles from anything. Its WalkScore? 0.

The third is called EcoSense—don't you love that name?—near Victoria, BC. Its WalkScore is all of 2 out of 100!

So added together, these three so-called "living buildings" have a combined WalkScore of 13.

Just for comparison, my own home in downtown Chicago has a WalkScore of 97. My home in downtown Memphis has a WalkScore of 89. So these "living buildings"—the epitome of green—are buildings that no one can get to without a car? C'mon. How sustainable can they be? Context, indeed, matters to a city's vitality, sustainability, and even innovation. Many scholars now make the case that the cycle of innovation must accelerate if we are to keep America competitive and replace depleting resources and obsolete ideas. But innovation relies on the collision of ideas and people. Innovation relies on happy accidents.

Unfortunately, mid-size, auto-dependent cities are at a disadvantage when it comes to producing happy accidents. Too few people, spread out over too much land, make it hard for people to find each other and much harder to find people with similar interests. The only hope of overcoming this disadvantage is to make great places that attract their unfair share of people.

The future of our cities demands new thinking. The worst thing we can do is to look at other successful cities, and then attempt to copy what they've done. As business strategist Gary Hamel says, if something is labeled as a best practice, you can be sure that it isn't. It's been far too widely promulgated to be best. The best practice is somewhere out on the edge of practice, not yet discovered, not yet acknowledged.

But while we shouldn't copy what others are doing, we can learn from it. Where would I start?

We could look at how Melbourne, Australia, essentially a suburban city, has attracted almost 100,000 new residents to its once sleepy central city in less than a decade. The city is adding Barcelona-style density to its "high streets," or streetcar corridors. There is still plenty of opportunity for suburban living in Melbourne. But now, the people there have another option—an urban option. With these bold moves, Melbourne has leapt out of nowhere onto everyone's list of world's top cities.

The challenge is to remake our cities in ways that will give them and their citizens the best chance for success. That means developing all of our talent and then holding on to it by making quality places.

Carol Coletta is president of Coletta & Company, a consulting firm leading the start-up of ArtPlace, a new initiative to spark creative placemaking across America. For the past six years, she was president and CEO of CEOs for Cities.

In addition, Coletta served as executive director of the Mayors' Institute on City Design, a partnership of the National Endowment for the Arts, U.S. Conference of Mayors and American Architectural Foundation. For 10 years, she was the host and producer of the nationally syndicated public radio show Smart City.

Coletta was a Knight Fellow in Community Building for 2003 at the University of Miami, School of Architecture. In 2010, she was named Honorary Senior Fellow of the Design Futures Council. In 2008, she was named one of the world's 50 most important urban experts by a leading European think tank and as one of the top 50 urban thinkers of all time by readers of Planetizen.com.

---

why the economics of "place" matters

DR. SOJI ADELAJA & MARK WYCKOFF

"Place" has always been important for sustained economic activity. Some prosperous places have taken advantage of unique location attributes (such as deep water close to shore, and available natural resources such as minerals) for over a thousand years. Other locations were picked for economic success based on similar characteristics, but for a variety of reasons failed to thrive. However, understanding what worked in the distant past is less complicated than understanding what works today. Although one observation is clear—the characteristics that made places successful have evolved over time as economies have changed. Our notions of place have also been refined as we learn more about the economics of place.

This chapter briefly explores the emerging science of place by first examining the difference between "place" and "Place" in geographic, economic development, and public policy contexts. It then examines the economics of place as contrasted between Old and New Economy views. Next, it turns to the characteristics of successful places that can be quantified and compared in the context of the global New Economy. The chapter concludes with examples of placemaking and place-based strategies to attract certain target populations and businesses, based on what we have learned from the emerging science of place.

Downtown Howell, Michigan. Courtesy of the Michigan Municipal League

DIFFERENCES BETWEEN "place" AND "Place"

Recently, there is increasing attention being paid to the term "place," and on what it means in a variety of contexts. For example:

- The term is typically used loosely and generally to describe a physical location or geography, such as the intersection of 5th and Oak Streets.

- It is also used to describe the attributes of a physical geography that makes a location interesting and visually attractive, such as a tree-lined street or a building with unique architectural features.

- More recently, the term "sense of place" is used to describe not so much physical geography or the attributes of that geography, but the emotional response one has to a special allure and warmth when at a location that has unique and attractive amenities. These attributes are often associated with public and private gathering places at which people are engaged in activities that are enjoyable, fun, or memorable; such as a public square for a speech by a famous person, a tavern with friends, or a cemetery visiting the grave of a loved one.

The most important contemporary context for "place" is its role in contributing to the economic development and prosperity of a community or region because of the ability of quality places to serve as attractors of talent and knowledge businesses. We refer to places in the typical geographic context as place with a lower case "p." We refer to places with allure that are created to attract people and businesses, to improve the quality of life and economic competitiveness as places with an upper case "P."

Lower case place is a geographic location that is often of little public note. That does not make it unimportant. The place could be where one lives, works, shops or goes to school. But, on its own, it does not serve as a significant attractor of people or businesses and there are few, if any, spinoff benefits. Upper case Place includes locations with a comprehensive set of attributes (including natural characteristics, built amenities, architectural design, people friendliness, etc.) and amenities that enhance a geographic location. In this instance, Place is a higher order concept that goes beyond locations and their attributes and includes the effects of all of those attributes on advancing specific human social, environmental and economic objectives. For example, an intersection of two streets and nothing else is a place. Add red brick apartment buildings, first-floor shops, and trees between the street and sidewalk and it is a place with specific characteristics. Add transit, bicycle paths, a park, a few restaurants with outdoor seating, pubs and people who come there because they want to be there and enjoy being there, and one has a special Place. At this point, a "critical mass" of features and amenities has been achieved in that Place. If a community has enough Places then the community itself becomes a special Place (such as Tucson, or New York City). If a region has enough Places then it becomes a special Place (e.g. Napa Valley).

"place" in Woodbridge, Michigan. Courtesy of www.pedbikeimages.org – Dan Burden

"Place" in Petoskey, Michigan. Courtesy of the Michigan Municipal League

Place has become an emerging central theme in state and federal policies. The issuance of a special joint memorandum by the White House Office of Management and Budget, Domestic Policy Council, Office of Urban Affairs and the National Economic Council (August 11, 2009, M-09-28) promoting place-based strategies for economic development, highlight the idea that place is not only an important underpinning concept for future economic development policies, but that prosperous Places can be created through the conscious act of "placemaking" in order to achieve various social, economic, environmental, and other objectives. As evidence of the commitment to this idea, the U.S. Department of Housing and Urban Development (HUD) has floated a series of competitive grant programs and major initiatives highlighting the notion of Place and signaling the validity of the placemaking concept. The HUD Neighborhood Stabilization Program (rounds 1 and 2, and most likely 3) leverage the Place concept in prescribing how federal investments are to be made. This leveraging is even more significant in the Partnership for Sustainable Communities program involving HUD, Department of Transportation, and the Environmental Protection Agency. Thus, in order for Michigan communities and regions to be competitive with other communities and regions across the nation for fiscal resources designed to help enhance economic activity, it is very important to understand the basic characteristics of not only places, but also of what can transform a place into a Place.

ECONOMICS OF "PLACE"

Economic theory provides us with a clear understanding of what place may have meant in the distant past and gives us insights into what it can mean for our future.

Economic prosperity has long been a central objective of societies. Indeed, for at least a century, much of the U.S. economy was based on the notion that successful Places became successful because they were able to generate significant economic activity, which invariably was tied to productive capacity. The traditional neoclassical economic growth models depicted place performance or outcomes (such as prosperity) as functions of a place's accumulation of capital, skilled labor, management, and natural resource base and accessibility. A place was considered to be a "good place" and likely a "prosperous place" in economic terms if it was abundant in each of these four inputs to the production process. In such neoclassical economic models, all other considerations were summed up under the category of intangibles. Critical place features such as woodland, wetlands, museums, entertainment facilities, wide choice in housing and transportation, etc., were considered intangible because they did not enter into the basic production structure through the four critical inputs to the production process.

Neoclassical theory did acknowledge the relationship between economic performance, as outcomes of productive input, and many of the amenities that society enjoyed in the past. The relationship was viewed in the context that economic prosperity enabled the building of amenities that in turn helped facilitate the productive prowess of a place.

Downtown Flint, Michigan. Courtesy of the Michigan Municipal League

In other words, it was a production-centric view. If one improves the quality of labor, management, access to natural resources, etc., then there would be more output or economic activity.

This model aptly described the economy of the past and the concept of place in the past. After all, the American economy was anchored by key production places (Detroit, Pittsburgh, Philadelphia, and Kansas City, for example) which leveraged the labor and natural assets of their locations and those of neighboring places to grow employment, population, income, and quality of life. These places were indeed prosperous. The implication is that prosperity and place were interchangeable—that a good place had the attributes to be an effective place in a production-based economy. We refer to this as the Manufacturing Economy, or the Old Economy. Detroit could be considered the poster child of the Old Economy.

The New Economy refers to a global, entrepreneurial, and knowledge-based economy where business success comes increasingly from the ability to incorporate knowledge, technology, creativity, and innovation into products and services.

The economy of today, referred to as the Knowledge Economy, or for our purposes, the New Economy, is built upon the Old Economy, but it also has other attributes. We will identify those shortly. The New Economy refers to a global, entrepreneurial, and knowledge-based economy where business success comes increasingly from the ability to incorporate knowledge, technology, creativity, and innovation into products and services.

So much has changed in the last several years in terms of the decline of manufacturing and other production-based activities (what people did with their hands and machines), that today's concept of Place in the New Economy is no longer the same as the traditional concept of place in the Old Economy. Now services, instead of manufacturing, have become more prominent in defining the economy of places. For example, the emergence of digital processing and communication now enables new products and services that do not need a traditional production pass-through to generate value. Models that once explained place in terms of the contribution of a physical location to traditional production and manufacturing are not so valid today.

Has the economy changed drastically? You bet! Table 1 illustrates the difference between places in the Old and New Economy. There are many place dimensions to these changes.

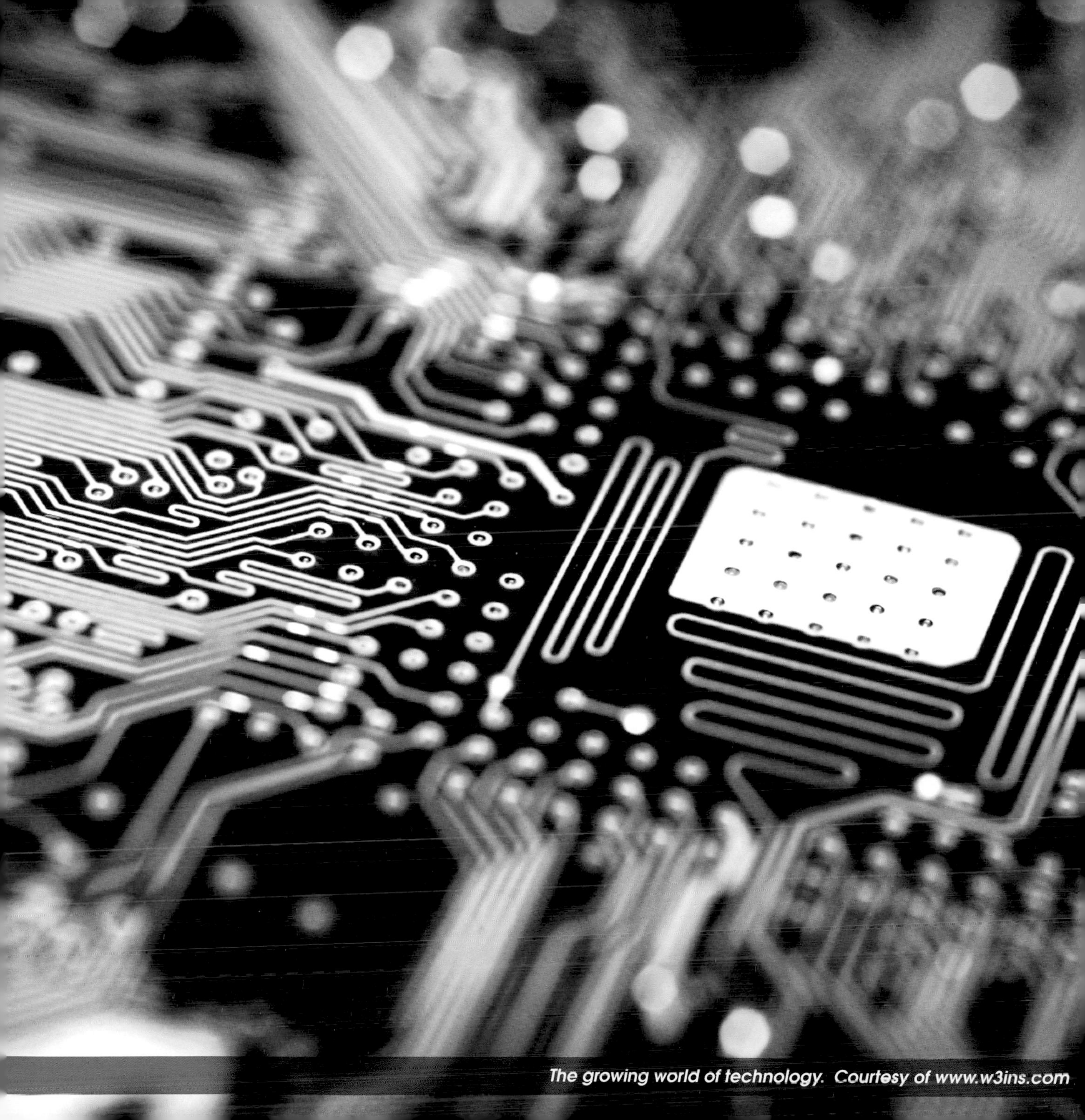
The growing world of technology. Courtesy of www.w3ins.com

A COMPARISON OF THE OLD ECONOMY AND NEW ECONOMY WITH RESPECT TO PLACE

KEY FEATURES OF THE OLD ECONOMY	KEY FEATURES OF THE NEW ECONOMY
Inexpensive place to do business was key.	Being rich in talent and ideas is key.
Attracting companies was key.	Attracting educated people is key.
A high-quality physical environment was a luxury, which stood in the way of attracting cost-conscious businesses.	Physical and cultural amenities are key in attracting knowledge workers.
Success = fixed competitive advantage in some resource or skill. The labor force was skills dependent.	Success = organizations and individuals with the ability to learn and adapt.
Economic development was government-led. Large government meant good services.	Bold partnerships with business, government, and nonprofit sector lead change.
Industrial sector (manufacturing) focus.	Sector diversity is desired, and clustering of related sectors is targeted.
Fossil fuel dependent manufacturing.	Communications dependent, but energy smart.
People followed jobs.	Talented, well-educated people choose location first, then look for or create a job.
Location mattered (esp. relative to transportation and raw materials).	Quality places with a high quality of life matter more.
Dirty, ugly, and a poor-quality environment were common outcomes that did not prevent growth.	Clean, green environment and proximity to open space and quality recreational opportunities are critical.
Connection to global opportunities not essential.	Connection to emerging global opportunities is critical.

Evidence of this shift from the Old to New Economy and its impact on our notions of place is overwhelming. But what is even more telling as to how the economy has changed is the range of attributes and amenities that researchers have identified as critical and necessary in order for economic activity or prosperity to happen. If Place connotes the combination of physical location, and the attributes of that location and how well those attributes are configured to drive such things as attractiveness to economic activity, and people allure, then the concept of Place today has changed, just as the Old Economy is morphing to the New Economy. Prosperous Places are not just GPS locations. They are destination points with unique assets and attributes, bustling communities, and in some cases, regions that everyone wants to be a part of.

Our notion of Place is not the static traditional notion, but is more reflective of a set of attributes and amenities that a place needs in order to be successful. This fits into the notion of placemaking, place-based strategies, and creating a sense of place. When we use these terms, we use them in the context of added amenities that are needed for a physical location to be functional, as well as attractive, and alluring. As a result, these Places are prosperous.

So our definition of Place is really about the amenities that are brought to a place beyond the traditional economic capital, such as human capital, social capital, and environmental capital. When the assets of a place are used to create new opportunities for human expression, such as through the arts; for human amusement, through socializing and entertainment; and for connecting back to nature, through our natural resources, then not only is the quality of life of everyone enhanced, the attractiveness of the place for economic activity, for job creation, for population attraction, and income growth are also enhanced.

CHARACTERISTICS OF SUCCESSFUL PLACES IN THE NEW ECONOMY

The challenge for most Midwestern communities is how to transform themselves from a position of prominence in the past, to being sufficiently prominent in the New Economy to be globally competitive.

A number of researchers have shed light on what it takes for communities to be successful today. Most of these studies have measured success on the basis of such things as job creation potential, income growth potential, people attraction potential, and company attraction potential.

These studies have helped identify key factors that drive jobs, incomes, and people to places. Among the factors they have identified as critical to the contemporary success of a place are the following:

- Human capital—not just skills but knowledge, the ability to create, and the ability to innovate as with the creative class (Lucas, 1988; Mathur, 1999; Rauch, 1993; Glaeser and Saiz, 2003);
- Knowledge infrastructure—educational institutions have been shown to contribute significantly to the income potential of communities around them (Peck, 2005; Friedman, 2002; McGranahan and Wojan, 2007; Sassen, 1994; Howkins, 2002; Castells, 1989; Wu, 2005; Etzkowitz et al, 2000);
- IT infrastructure—including broadband (Kellerman, 2000 and 2002; Webster, 2006; Castells, 2000);
- Museums, cultural and social amenities (Clark, 2003; Florida, 2000 and 2005; Gottlieb, 2003);
- Parks, trails, green space and other green infrastructure (Deller et al, 2001; McGranahan, 1999; Scott, 2000);
- Rivers, lakes, ponds and other blue infrastructure (Deller et al, 2001; McGranahan and Wojan, 2007; English, 2000; Clark, 2004);
- Weather and climate (not just warm and sunny) (Barro and Sala-i-Martin, 1991);
- Regional strategies and interrelationships (Weinert, 2002; Bartik, 1997; Santos, 1998; Alderman, 1998; Azfar et al, 2000);
- Economic gardening and entrepreneurship (Hackler, 2003; Lichtenstein and Lyons, 2006; Goetz and Freshwater, 2001);
- Venture capital (Abrams, 1999);
- Formation of interlinked economic clusters and agglomeration (Feser and Bergman, 2000; Watts, 2000; Sadler, 2004).

(For full citations and a more comprehensive listing of studies related to specific factors and their authors, see Adelaja et al, *Chasing the Past or Investing in Our Future*, 2009; or contact the authors.)

The evidence from research has not only identified many of the elements of success of a location, it has shown links between the above factors. Recent research by the Michigan State University Land Policy Institute (LPI) shows that it is the combination and agglomeration of factors that result in benefits. One of the more recent LPI studies essentially threw as many of these factors into a new endogenous growth economic model, aiming to give every proposed driver of prosperity an equal chance of being detected as relevant. Rather than tying everything to production, many factors or amenities can help shape the result and the model attempts to measure them. The results showed how

Whirlpool Compass Fountain, St. Joseph, Michigan. Courtesy of the Michigan Municipal League

each of these factors contributes not only to employment, income, and population, but also revealed the specific role of subcomponents, such as differential effects of specific age groups. The findings also reveal how much the economy has changed and how the former intangibles have now become the tangibles.

A more contemporary theory of place, place performance and prosperity, and therefore, what a place has to do to be successful in the New Economy, can be captured in a new simplified model of growth. This model builds on the old neoclassical economic growth models, but the requirements for place performance exceed capital, skilled labor, management, and natural resource base and accessibility. The contemporary model includes such new factors as venture capital, talent, innovative capacity, entrepreneurial capacity, natural amenities, urban amenities, social capital, digital communication capacity, creativity, and others.

So Place and placemaking not only involve more options in terms of what places can do to achieve prosperity, but include elements that were not relevant in the past. These new elements represent opportunities to make significant advancements in place performance. So what is a Place? In this context, a Place is a particular physical location characterized by a strong concentration of these relevant (many formerly intangible) factors or amenities (based on the authentic assets of a place) that are assembled at, constructed in, or attracted to that location in order to be more competitive in the global New Economy.

What people are looking for today are not simply places; they want Places. These are different than those in the Old Economy, because the world economy has changed. The research highlights the notion that the knowledge and creative class that are critical drivers of prosperity in the New Economy, tend to look for many of these new attributes and pursue them. Jobs follow due to their creative capacity and the ability of the Place to attract the people and businesses that create the jobs. Essentially, the amenities of the Place help to make it become a "job factory." This helps to clarify an important distinction that must be made in understanding place. That is the distinction between a physical building, or real estate concept of place, and the concept of sense of place, a community of place, and a region that has regional place persona.

So, placemaking to create New Economy Places can take different contexts depending on what the objective is:

Creating a particular type of Place because of its economic benefits, such as:

- Creating an attractive downtown,
- Creating a nice vacation destination,
- Conceptualizing a city of the future that attracts jobs/opportunities, or
- Repositioning a region to be relevant in the global New Economy.

Creating a Place that is attractive to a particular age demographic, occupation, or business set, such as:

- Creative and talented 25 to 34 year olds,
- Middle age, family-raising knowledge workers,
- Immigrants, or
- Pre-retirees.

We advocate not only community placemaking, but more importantly, regional placemaking, based on the notion that the most globally alluring assets have at least a regional dimension. Places within a region that are cooperatively working together to be globally competitive are more likely to succeed than working alone or competing for a larger piece of a fixed pie. Major lakes, world-class universities, emerging business clusters, large numbers of talented people, great health care, and regional high-speed transit are all examples of assets that can be used to create globally competitive regions. This type of placemaking also avoids Peter from robbing Paul (e.g. East Lansing benefiting at the expense of Lansing by enticing a business to move from one to the other). In a global sense, all communities in a region are neighbors and allies. Competitors are elsewhere in the world. New residents and new businesses that come to a region benefit everyone in the region, not just the community in which they locate. The synergistic effect of multiple communities working together to achieve regional competitiveness, by creating Places that are attractive to new people, new talent, and new knowledge businesses, is much greater and more powerful than any community could ever achieve working alone.

EXAMPLES OF PLACEMAKING AND PLACE-BASED STRATEGIES FOR PROSPERITY

We know enough from emerging research to know generally those features and amenities that interest different segments of the population in large cities, suburbs, and small communities. We also know the net economic impacts of these population segments. This provides us with a better opportunity to target particular populations that have great economic expansion potential, with placemaking improvements that are attractive to those populations, while also creating more Places that are globally competitive. The following table provides examples of SOME of the placemaking improvements that can turn a place into Place.

EXAMPLES OF PLACEMAKING AND PLACE-BASED STRATEGIES

DENSE LARGE CITY

TARGET POPULATION	EXISTING CONDITIONS	STRATEGIC IMPROVEMENTS
Young creative talent (Ages 25-34) These are usually creative and well-educated single people establishing their first households. They spend a lot and eat out frequently. They like a wide variety of arts and entertainment opportunities. They often do not own cars and may prefer to use public transit if available. They are also at that point in life when their innovative and entrepreneurial ambitions first get expressed.	Downtown has little housing and little variety in evening activities. May be a large daytime population, but has little activity after the workday ends. Large amount of underutilized land and land in parking lots; many opportunities for infill development and to increase downtown density and intensity of use all day and evening.	Create a wide range of housing opportunities: Stimulate warehouse conversions to lofts, convert old hotels and offices to condominiums, construction of one and two bedroom apartments. Create a wide range of entertainment and eating establishment options. Improve external appearance and maintenance of cultural attractions and entertainment areas and beef up security. Improve transit service. Create more bike paths and links to parks, green and blue infrastructure. Provide incubators and entrepreneurship services. Leverage existing incentive programs to target new development that would attract the target population while also achieving broader community benefits.
Immigrants (wide range of ages and cultural backgrounds)	Few places in the metro area with the characteristics they seek: dense, small homes and lots, good transit, and neighborhood shopping within walking distance.	Support concentrations of immigrant populations in neighborhoods with desired characteristics. Implement neighborhood stabilization programs. Targeted first home loan programs. Improve transit service. Provide incubators and entrepreneurship services.

TO ATTRACT CERTAIN TARGET POPULATIONS AND BUSINESSES

DENSE LARGE CITY CONTINUED

TARGET POPULATION	EXISTING CONDITIONS	STRATEGIC IMPROVEMENTS
Knowledge workers (Ages 35-54) This group is well educated and has started families so few will remain downtown. They want a range of housing in neighborhoods near downtown and other job centers, as well as near family shopping venues. Highly educated and creative knowledge immigrants also fall into this category.	A range of residential neighborhoods including small starter homes, fixer uppers, and large historic homes in stabilizing neighborhoods. Nearby neighborhood shopping. Little opportunity for networks and entrepreneurial collaboration.	Significant efforts to improve the quality of public schools and to engage neighborhoods in their improvement. Strong neighborhood watch and community policing initiatives. Significant incentives to improve neighborhood shopping districts. Provide incubators and entrepreneurship services. Facilitate community organized business and professional networks. Improve transit service. Create more bike paths and links to parks, green and blue infrastructure.
Pre-retirees (Ages 55-64) This group is downsizing housing and likes a vibrant downtown with many cultural and entertainment options.	Downtown has little housing and little variety in evening activities.	Same strategies as for 25-34, and 35-54 year olds; especially as relates to dining, entertainment, parks, walkability and community safety.

SUBURBAN CITY OR TOWNSHIP

TARGET POPULATION	EXISTING CONDITIONS	STRATEGIC IMPROVEMENTS
Young creative talent (Ages 25-34)	This group mostly grew up in the suburbs and would rather live downtown in the nearby big city—until they pair up and start to have children and decide to move to the suburbs for better schools and homes with yards. Lack of specific amenities may impair their choice to stay in the suburbs.	Improve transportation options, especially transit, between the suburb and their jobs downtown. Loans for first-time home buyers. Neighborhood stabilization programs. Improve restaurant and entertainment options at key nodes. Build infill housing with greater variety of types. Attract mixed-use developments along major corridors and at key nodes. Create more bike paths and links to parks, green and blue infrastructure both within the suburb and connect to more urban and more rural places a few miles away.

TO ATTRACT CERTAIN TARGET POPULATIONS AND BUSINESSES

SUBURBAN CITY OR TOWNSHIP CONTINUED

TARGET POPULATION	EXISTING CONDITIONS	STRATEGIC IMPROVEMENTS
Knowledge workers (Ages 35-54) Raising well-educated families is what they do when not working.	This group is for the most part, already well served by the suburbs which were designed for them. They appreciate the wealth of jobs and other opportunities that a large city and its suburbs provide, but, the suburbs may be "boring" and they do not like the time delay and stress associated with suburb-to-suburb traffic movement and the lack of intergovernmental infrastructure cooperation.	Maintain good schools. Provide a wide range of sports at good recreational facilities and other activities for youth and families. Maintain good shopping areas. Improve transit service. Attract mixed-use developments along major corridors and at key nodes. Create more bike paths and links to parks, green and blue infrastructure both within the suburb and connect to more urban and more rural places a few miles away. Target regional scale quality of life improvements that cannot go downtown such as major airports, amusement parks, regional scale parks, certain sports teams, etc.
Pre-retirees (Ages 55-64)	Few apartments and elderly housing complexes. Few restaurant and leisurely dining establishments.	Improve transit service. Increase apartment and elderly housing options. Increase dining establishments. Attract mixed-use developments along major corridors and at key nodes. Create more bike paths and links to parks, green and blue Infrastructure both within the suburb and connect to more urban and more rural places a few miles away.

RURAL TOWN

TARGET POPULATION	EXISTING CONDITIONS	STRATEGIC IMPROVEMENTS
Young creative talent (Ages 25-34) Something special about this place attracted them here. Could be family, a family business, natural environment, recreational opportunities, or other unique features. But these need to be identified and used to market the place to others with similar interests. Early engagement to a service business and then to the entire area.	If based on farming or forestry, the town probably appears "tired and in need of sprucing up." If based on tourism, may already look pretty good and have more amenities than other towns its size because of the larger population served during peak seasons. Opportunities for entrepreneurial development is limited.	Create a wider range of entertainment and eating establishment options. Provide incubators and entrepreneurship services. Create more bike paths and links to parks, green and blue infrastructure both within the town and connect to rural places a few miles away. Improve broadband and cell phone communication capacity.

TO ATTRACT CERTAIN TARGET POPULATIONS AND BUSINESSES

RURAL TOWN CONTINUED

TARGET POPULATION	EXISTING CONDITIONS	STRATEGIC IMPROVEMENTS
Knowledge workers (Ages 35-54) Raising families and enjoying the rural environment is what they do when not working.	If based on farming or forestry, the town probably appears "tired and in need of sprucing up." If based on tourism, may already look pretty good and have more amenities than other towns its size because of the larger population served during peak seasons. Opportunities for entrepreneurial development is limited.	Maintain good schools. Neighborhood stabilization programs. Provide a wide range of activities for youth and families. Maintain good shopping areas. Construct small mixed-use developments in key activity locations. Develop regional nodes of activity. Seek game changing connections with distant cities, universities, and hospitals, etc. Provide continuing education and workforce development opportunities.
Pre-retirees (Ages 55-64)	Same as cell above, plus Few apartments and elderly housing complexes.	Improve bus service. Increase apartment and elderly housing options, including construction of retirement communities. Attract mixed-use developments along major corridors and at key nodes. Create more bike paths and links to parks, green and blue infrastructure, both within the town and connect to rural places a few miles away.

SUMMARY

So in a nutshell, Place is a complex concept that connotes the empowerment of communities whose vision of future prosperity is built on effectively utilizing their unique assets to attract new people and new economic activity. It also connotes the notion that authenticity and uniqueness are important. Many of the assets that communities need to work with are different from the assets that worked well for success in the past. We are in a New Economy where the framework for prosperity and placemaking must reflect contemporary knowledge of what works and what does not. It is important to recognize that the remarkable shift in what factors are relevant today, compared to the past, requires a change in mindset. If a community adheres to old principles as to how prosperity materializes, it is likely that it would be relying on policies that are no longer valid. Many of Michigan's communities are still using tools of the last half-century to achieve Old Economy outcomes that are no longer relevant in the global New Economy. Communities must remain adaptable with the ability to change over time or else they will shrink and die. Adherence to Place factors that are relevant in the New Economy when designing and implementing place-based improvements will help ensure that individual communities, and the regions they are in, remain competitive in the face of changing global economic conditions. The authors hope the information in this chapter points the way for more prosperous Places at the community and regional level in Michigan.

Dr. Soji Adelaja is the John A. Hannah Professor in Land Policy at Michigan State University (MSU) and is the founder of the MSU Land Policy Institute. His faculty appointment is in the department of Agricultural, Food and Resource Economics. Until April 2011, he served as the director of the Land Policy Institute at MSU, which he founded in 2006; as co-director of the W.K. Kellogg Foundation-funded People and Land Initiative (PAL); and as the director of Michigan Higher Education Land Policy Consortium (MIHELP) which he founded in 2005. Dr. Adelaja is now spearheading new initiatives in international land use. An eclectic scholar and team-builder, his research and outreach programs span a variety of areas, including the areas of land use, land policy, renewable energy, metropolitan growth strategies, both place and prosperity science, regional prosperity strategies and growth modeling in the New Economy, and political economy modeling.

Mark Wyckoff is widely considered an expert on Michigan land use law and on statewide land use trends and land use policy. He is a frequent workshop and conference speaker, and is widely consulted on pending legislative issues by a wide range of stakeholder groups, including state legislators and nonprofit advocacy organizations. Wyckoff served with associates of Public Sector Consultants as staff to the Michigan Land Use Leadership Council in 2003. He is a fellow of the American Institute of Certified Planners, director of the Planning and Zoning Center at Michigan State University, and senior associate director of the Land Policy Institute.

building place: the key to healthy, sustainable communities

DAN BURDEN

Late fall brought me to New York City where I had the good fortune to meet long-time friend, Tony Hiss, a retired writer and editor for *The New Yorker*, and author of 13 books. It was Tony who inspired me as a young professional. His book, *The Experience of Place*, not only influenced me, but also encouraged many great city makers. Jane Jacobs, urban writer and activist, who describes the essence of cities, shared her inspirations with Tony, and he with her.

We decided to meet at Grand Central Station and there, tucked in the center of humanity, Tony and I discussed many things as we watched people going places. We marveled at the elaborate dance going on around us as that day's half a million travelers moved through the station, accommodating one another. In the heart of one of the world's greatest cities, in its central transportation hub, we watched un-choreographed movement—strangers anticipating and responding to one another—as they went on their way. All age groups were present and the continuous stream of travelers arriving and departing kept a remarkably consistent pace—something that could never happen on any freeway. This great hall, inspired and adorned by artisans, moves more people than Los Angeles' top two freeways combined.

In his newest book, *In Motion: The Experience of Travel*, Tony examines the meaning of travel in our lives. Beginning with the etymology of travel, Tony goes back to its Old French form "traveillier," which is associated with toil, trouble, and torment. I nod as he tells me this, thinking of the modern commuter stuck in rush-hour traffic, the miles of queuing, brake lights, and the stress we are all under as we compare the time in the vehicle with the distance traveled. In the past three decades, we have grown traffic five times faster than we have grown our population, I tell Tony, but our network of new streets has increased by 5 percent. Given these figures, the torment of travel is likely to get worse for many. Americans have expressed their angst and displeasure; collectively we spend more minutes on our commute than on our vacations. This eats away at everything we do, including how much time we spend as volunteers.

Bikers participating in the Tour de Troit, Detroit, Michigan. Courtesy of the Michigan Municipal League

As far back as 1086 in England, in an ambitious census, it was recorded that those who worked away from home needed 20 minutes to reach their fields or pastures. There must be magic in this number. Even today, this is close to our average commute time (25.1 minutes, each way). During our conversation, Tony speaks of making all trips richer experiences. I agree. Research shows that driving to work keeps blood pressure elevated for two hours afterwards. A walk or bike ride, on the other hand, is good for the heart.

PLACE AFFECTS WHO WE ARE

Our conversation has this ebb and flow—friends sharing the details of their work with one another and recognizing the similarities that bolster and validate what the other has been doing. In the anteroom of Grand Central Station's Oyster Bar, Tony whispers into the wall and his voice carries to where I stand, despite the dozens of people between us. Surrounded by thoughtful, inspiring, functioning design, Tony says,

"The places where we spend our time affect the people we are and who we become." He later adds, "The relationship with the places we know...is a close bond...a continuum with all we are."

I believe this is true.

Opposite Page: "The Rapid", Grand Rapid's Public Bus Route Map. Courtesy of The Rapid

After lunch, we began walking around the city. As we walked, we talked about the influencers of cities. Tony, William Hollingsworth "Holly" Whyte, an American urbanist, and Jane Jacobs focused their writing on place and profoundly influenced planners and designers—though they were not planners or designers. Holly, an observer of life, described in detail how and why we use spaces the way we do—the open space between buildings, streets, parks, plazas, parking lots. Jane, taking inspiration from Holly, dove into the complexities, joys, delights, and gifts of a functioning city. She noted how urban renewal experts, people with shallow insights, experts in only one field, and many others who didn't even care about where people lived, or how, became the destroyers of cities. Through careless planning, the life went out of some great cities. Jane, Holly, and Tony, the great defenders of place, remind me that each of us—every person, no matter the background—can improve where and how we live.

As I walked through the city with Tony, then later with my 26-year-old daughter, Juli, I was introduced to lively and quiet places, some of their favorite spots. We visited High Line Park, one of the newest places in the city, where a raised freight line, abandoned decades ago, has been transformed into a park filled with people—children playing, lovers holding hands, and people watching people, all enjoying being there. Below, Chelsea Market bustles with activity.

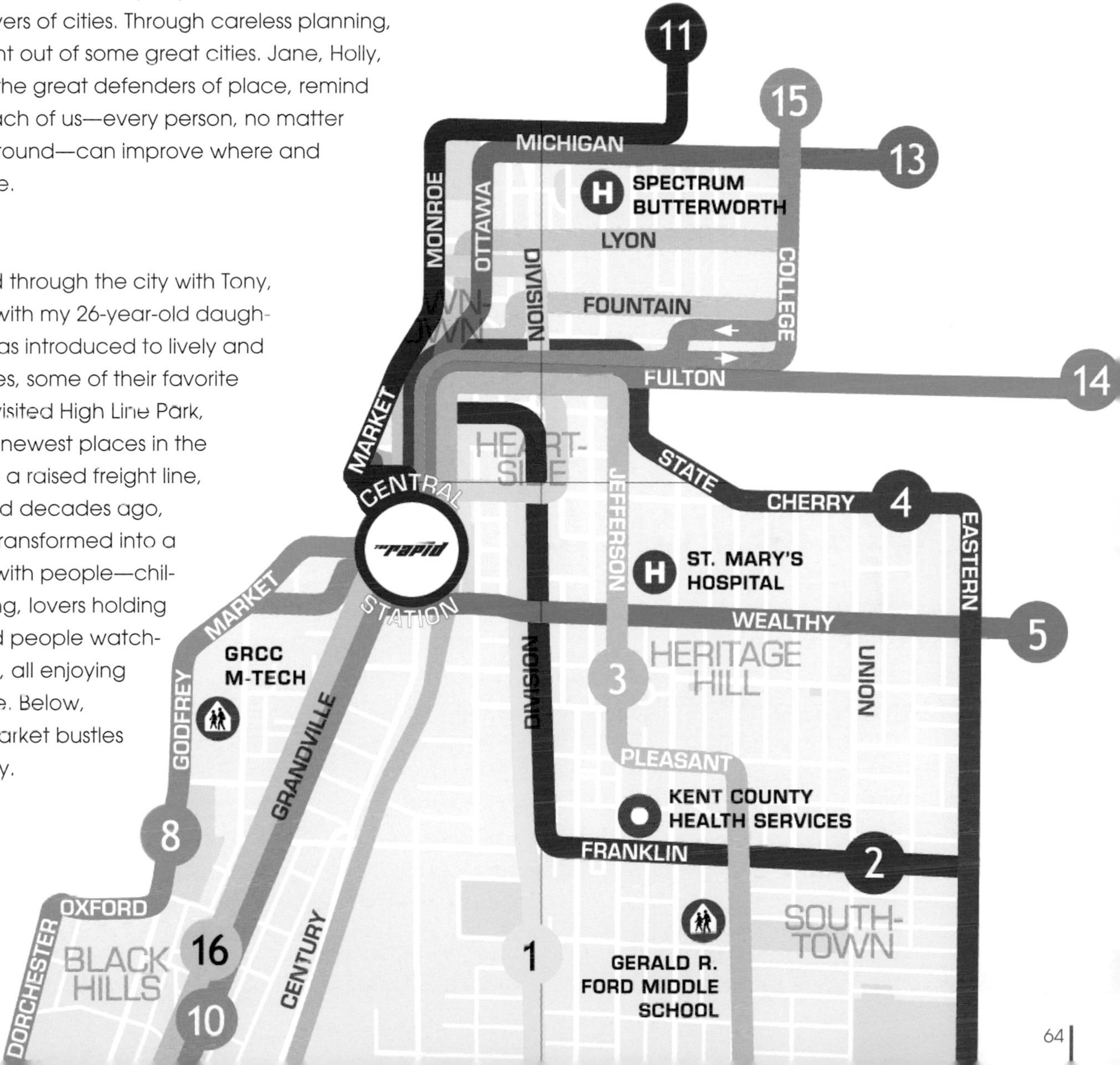

THE HIGH LINE SUCCESS STORY

The story of the park is a wonderful one. The High Line was originally constructed in the 1930s to take freight trains off Manhattan's streets. The park is owned by the city of New York and operated under the jurisdiction of the New York City Department of Parks & Recreation, but it is the "Friends of the High Line," citizens and activists, who raised the private funds for the park and who oversee its maintenance and operations through an agreement with the parks department. When all sections are complete, the High Line will be a mile-and-a-half-long elevated park, running through the west side neighborhoods of the Meatpacking District, West Chelsea, and Clinton/Hell's Kitchen. It features meandering pathways, natural plantings, seating, and lighting, and it is another example of people making a difference in their community. Friends of the High Line was founded in 1999 by two neighborhood residents, Joshua David and Robert Hammond, who advocated for the High Line's preservation when the structure was under threat of demolition. They worked with Mayor Michael Bloomberg and the New York City council to reverse a city policy of demolition to ensure preservation of the High Line through the federal Rail-Banking program. They also spearheaded the design process for the High Line's transformation into a public park. As they did this, they included access points from the street level every two to three blocks with elevators and stairs for maximum accessibility. The park and the market, adjacent land forms where one is literally above the other, complement each other, provide balance, and offer an outstanding example of residents taking the initiative to improve quality of life for all.

CITIZENS AND GOVERNMENTS ARE BOTH RESPONSIBLE

I have worked with 3,000 communities in North America, 224 communities and neighborhoods in Michigan, and have learned that we build our streets, villages, townships, cities and regions in three ways. First, we examine the design side of things—integrating land use and transportation. We maximize sustainability, livability, quality of life, and prosperity when we explore the form, function, and character of our adjacent land uses because these things are intrinsically linked. Our block structures, patterns, and layout influence whether people will interact or not—how much time people will spend in cars or outdoors conversing with neighbors. Secondly, and this is the part that is almost wholly overlooked, we engage the public in a meaningful way. We do not just invite the public into the process; we understand that citizens are the community's greatest resource. Often the best ideas, the ones that have preservation and enhancement at their center, come from the community. Government alone cannot improve quality of life. Each human being has a responsibility to look around and note what works and what does not. Finally, the third step, implementation, reveals the quality of the first two. If the design or the public processes have been shoddy, this is exposed. At best, we have built compromise.

The High Line, New York, New York. Courtesy of the Michigan Municipal League

It was back in 1996 when I looked around in disbelief at the careless manner in which we were developing lands. Sprawl yawned across the American landscape. The consequences were numerous and ugly—strip malls, vacated downtowns, long commutes, higher obesity rates, an increase in the number and severity of traffic accidents, segregated housing, reduced personal time, and an overall isolation that was destroying communities and turning us into a population of strangers living in proximity to one another. Communities were unraveling as we were becoming increasingly secluded and locked away in our personal vehicles and single family homes.

I began working with local governments who realized that their development practices were unsustainable and that the costs associated with maintaining sprawl were destroying budgets. I focused on walkability. Walkability is the extent to which the built environment is friendly to the presence of people walking, living, shopping, visiting, and spending time in an area. A walkable community is one that allows us to access amenities by walking, and this is important because walking remains the cheapest form of transport. The construction of a walkable community provides the most affordable transportation system any community can plan, design, construct, and maintain. We know that walkable communities enable social interaction, encourage physical fitness, and protect our natural resources through sustainable practices. Other benefits often include lower crime rates, higher property values, cleaner air, and a stronger sense of community.

Built to a human scale—the foot—walkable communities are compact, and they place a person at the center of design. The result is an environment where all can live, work, play, and learn. Walkable communities maximize social engagement—they encourage activity and wellness, they work for children, seniors, and everyone in-between, and they rely on human beings instead of vehicles as the organizing principle. This is the heart of social equity; our communities work no matter what we earn or what we can afford to buy. Compact design also requires fewer miles of roads, sewers, utilities, and other infrastructure, and allows us to be efficient in our development practices.

ENGAGING CITIZENS

A recent study by the University of New Hampshire reveals, "In the age of increasing energy costs and climate considerations, the ability to walk to important locations is a key component of sustainable communities." While the benefits to our physical health and the environmental implications of walkable communities continue to be studied, the social benefits have not been investigated broadly. In *The Connected Community: Local Governments as Partners in Citizen Engagement and Community Building,* Arizona State University researchers note that civic engagement is either normative, based on the idea that building citizenship and community is important for its own sake, or instrumental, aimed at the approval or implementation of a particular policy or project. Community is defined as "the social connections of people who feel that they have some common characteristics and who are aware of and care about each other's welfare." Similarly, the International City/County Management Association's 2009 IQ Report noted com-

Civic engagement, Sylvan Lake, Michigan. Courtesy of the Michigan Municipal League munity as "characterized by a feeling of belonging, of pride, of being part of something important, of being included and not being alone." Researchers also noted that population distribution patterns over the past half century have weakened community ties and the sense of attachment we have to where we live. They also recognize, "It is hard to have citizen engagement without a sense of community, and it is hard to fashion a sense of community without citizen engagement."

Each community has its own degree of readiness in dealing with the consequences of sprawl. In the white paper, "What Is Social Capital and Why Does it Matter?", Dr. John C. Thomas states that social capital refers to "community connectedness," with components of 1) social networks—the extent to which people are involved with other people in social networks; and 2) feelings about reciprocity and trust—feelings that can grow from involvement in social networks. In his research, he notes that social capital promotes higher educational achievement, more effective governments, faster economic growth, and less crime and violence. By being accessible, honest, forthcoming with information, and by creating an engaging public process, the community feels heard from the outset. This allows government agencies to both perpetuate feelings of trust and help channel energy for the greatest good.

How do we encourage citizen engagement and build social capital? Citizen engagement, historically, has been focused on an exchange of information. The community is invited in when administrators decide that input is needed, or when it is mandated by law, at public hearings, citizen advisory councils, or during a public comment session. In *Public Deliberation: The Managers Guide to Civic Engagement*, Torres and Lukensmeyer (2006), researchers state, "the most successful citizen participation efforts today are those that understand engagement as a series of interrelated, developmental choices that have more to do with 'what level of involvement' along the policy development-implementation continuum than any single technique for 'one-off' events that fulfill statutory requirement." Instead of offering a robust public engagement process, many local governments have become "a broker for all information in techniques where people don't get to hear each other's point of view." Yet, a successful public engagement process requires that we 1) clearly state the agenda for a policy or program; 2) provide rationale for where the public will and won't be involved in the process; 3) address key issues upfront—budgetary or scheduling constraints, for example; 4) ask the community for the engagement techniques that will work best for them; and 5) justify the community engagement techniques throughout. Anything short of this breeds mistrust and discontentment.

Revitalizing buildings with art, Detroit, Michigan. Courtesy of the Michigan Municipal League

THE MICHIGAN EXPERIENCE

Across the nation, fringe development has led to vacated downtown centers. This coring of our communities as a result of sprawling land development patterns has eroded place. It is this loss of identity that every community should ultimately fear. As communities become big box stores strung along major transportation corridors, uniqueness is lost, place is lost. Serious consequences ensue. Today, we know that Michigan's faltering economy preceded the nation's plunge into this economic downturn. In Michigan, we over-relied on our transportation industry, both in the production of vehicles and by building roadways that did not help build communities, and induced massive sprawl. We disinvested in our center cities, and invested in an easy auto-supported flight to empty places—our new suburban pattern fully dependent on easy and cheap auto travel. Instead of building economic diversity and strength, we built traffic and dependency. Detroit, Flint, and Saginaw are now symbols of how avoiding basic principles in city-making leads to vast consumption of open land, longer commute times, less vacation time to enjoy these surroundings, a crumbling economy, and heavy auto dependence.

In 2010, I worked in Douglas, Durand, Fenton, Harbor Springs, Elk Rapids, Clare, Big Rapids, Fremont, Grand Haven, Lathrup Village, Lapeer, Linden, Spring Lake, Walker, Mt. Pleasant, Grandville, Allegan, Detroit, Tecumseh, Jonesville, Delta Township, Saginaw, Burton, Newberry, Sault Ste. Marie, Oxford, Holland, and Frankenmuth, Michigan. These communities are addressing complex land development and transportation planning issues—a historic highway bisecting the community; a failing Main Street; speeding vehicles in neighborhoods and school zones; lack of pedestrian and bicycling facilities; limited network and connectivity; peak hour congestion; sprawling development; and overly wide intersections, among other issues. In each of these cases, the land development patterns and the transportation systems are out of alignment—something has gone awry—resulting in significant impacts on the community. This is demonstrated through repeated bad behavior on the part of drivers—speeding, shortcuts through neighborhoods, general aggressiveness—and in other cases, the whole heart of a community, its economic center, has been cut from the community it was meant to serve.

The good news is that each of the communities understands that they must address land use and transportation together if they are to thrive. Michigan communities must strive to be efficient, effective, and holistic in what they do. They must take on the role of change agents to overcome the lethargy of ho-hum in governance, in order to meet the public as they push back for efficient and responsive governance, to address the corporate, Main Street, and Wall Street failings, and address the lost social capital. In many of these communities, I am reminded that our response to the conditions we have created will not be solved by one person or one administration acting alone. AmericaSpeaks, a Washington D.C.-based nonprofit organization whose mission is to "engage citizens in the public decisions that impact their lives," captures it best when they claim that "placing citizens closer to the affairs of government strengthens representation, transparency, and accountability, and can improve results."

The author conducting a walkability audit, Linden, Michigan. Courtesy of the Michigan Municipal League

Examples of this desire to better address land use are already coming from Michigan communities. When I think of the tough task all administrators and elected leaders face daily, I want to share the stories of those Michiganders who have inspired and emboldened me. Rich Morrison is one. When Rich and I first met, he was the community development and economic director for Brighton. Their historic main street had to carry a heavy load of traffic, 21,000 vehicles, in two lanes. An active rail line and a high school both complicated this by sending in surges of stored cars. Standing on a corner in Brighton with Rich, then-Mayor Kate Lawrence, then-Police Chief Mike Kinaschuk, City Manager Dana Foster, city council members, Downtown Development Authority members, planning commissioners, engineers, residents and city staff, I suggested two tools to honor the neighborhood, a roundabout to address the traffic, and a pedestrian island near the high school. The elected and volunteer boards were supportive of these suggestions and the city council was bold in taking the lead and moving these projects to implementation. Today, the roundabout is a place of immense beauty and a source of pride for the community. It honors the neighborhood, helps pedestrians, keeps motorists flowing gently but quietly, and sets the tone of expectancy among all motorists in downtowns.

At the time we envisioned this design, it was a bold move—an untested career maker or breaker. We all knew this. Though Rich will point to all of those around him who made these things happen, he is largely responsible for the success. I have observed his approach in Mt. Pleasant where he rallies residents, staff, business leaders, and activists, and seeks out experts to complement the resources the community already has. This approach builds social capital and also allows for the most efficient and cost-effective form of government.

THE HAMBURG EXAMPLE

Rich also traveled to Hamburg, New York, to learn from one of the most significant transportation re-creations I have had the honor to be a part of—the $23 million reconstruction of U.S. Route 62 in the village of Hamburg, which received the Innovative Management Award as part of the American Transportation Award series. The reconstruction of Route 62 needed to address severe safety, capacity, and infrastructure deficiencies within the village. This route functioned as both a major truck route and the main street for the village. I worked with residents, business owners, and the New York Department of Transportation (NYDOT) to craft a workable vision that met the village's needs and met NYDOT's desire to keep traffic moving as they rebuilt three of the village's principal roads. The collaborative teamwork between the agency and the community resulted in well-informed and community-valued design alternatives, and it created close bonds with the community that are still strong today. The results of the reconstruction are stunning. Accidents have been dramatically reduced in the corridor, congestion has been minimized, and social capital has been increased. Rich visited Hamburg during an event in which current and former village staff, NYDOT, the police and fire departments, business leaders, school officials, and residents were celebrating how the design created place as opposed to destroying it. This example points to Rich's desire to make an informed decision by seeking out information both near and far, and in this process, building community. He witnessed the fruits of the robust public engagement process that was used in Hamburg.

Pedestrians utilizing a roundabout, Brighton, Michigan. Courtesy of www.pedbikeimages.org - Dan Burden

LET'S USE THE RIGHT PUBLIC ENGAGEMENT STRATEGIES

It is clear that in addition to building unhealthy communities, we have also been using the wrong public engagement strategies and techniques. Many decisions have been made in public hearing formats, which turn into screaming matches that bring out the worst in people. The methods used in Hamburg, New York, and Brighton, Michigan, brought out the best in people. Hamburg residents pored over aerial maps of their village, while the consultants stood back observing. It was the residents who drew meaningful new lines, found ways to get in more parking, identified the best new places for buildings, and agreed on which intersections needed roundabouts. The consultants and technical experts answered questions, provided training on placemaking and offered examples of best practices, but the community made the choices as a community. In Brighton, the methods were similar but enhanced by walking audits where we assessed the corridor as a community and envisioned the future together.

We have to be leaders in creating great streets, great neighborhoods, and great places of the heart. We need to start building our communities for and by people to accommodate vehicles—not just for vehicles. In his books, *The Rise of the Creative Class* and *Who's Your City?*, economist Richard Florida writes, "Place is becoming more relevant to the global economy and our individual lives. The choice of where to live, therefore, is not an arbitrary one. It is arguably the most important decision we make, as important as choosing a spouse or a career. In fact, place exerts powerful influence over the jobs and careers we have access to, the people we meet and our 'mating markets', and our ability to lead happy and fulfilled lives."

Thinking back to the day I spent with Tony in New York City, I sent him an email because I wanted his take on the following question: How do we create place? He writes, "Place, to me, is all about connectedness, which means strengthening people's connections to each other and to the larger family of fellow creatures with whom we share the planet—and simultaneously enlarging people's capacity to sense and be aware of these connections. This is what grounds us and provides the kind of stickiness (and stick-to-it-ive-ness) that holds us to a particular community. It's a process that works through physical interventions, through concerted social actions, and through changes in awareness all at the same time. To become a place, a community takes on the goal of stimulating the kinds of contacts between people that promote opportunities for caring, cooperating, creative solutions, common purpose, and mutual respect, and that foster the ability to sense and cherish these interactions whenever they occur. Physical locations that serve these functions become the sacred sites of a community; a healthy community has established an enveloping, unobtrusive, and entirely non-coercive network of sacred sites that throw people together and keep re-mixing them day after day." As usual, Tony makes me smile.

Creating social connections through walkability, Holland, Michigan. Courtesy of www.pedbikeimages.org - Dan Burden

BUILD PLACE NOT PROJECTS

Michigan stands out in my mind among all the rest as this nation's great hope for the future. Michigan is chock-full of great communities with the right pattern and scale to develop walkable, livable communities and to begin to re-create place. We can do this by bringing back a mix of land uses, adding density, focusing on infill development, and creating a built environment that is supportive of local economies and local jobs. It was the people and state of Michigan that changed transportation in this country and Michigan will do it again. The focus this time will be on multi-modal transportation because when a place invites us to switch modes seamlessly—to choose walking, biking, transit, or driving to reach a destination—we know that the transportation system and land uses are in balance. They are working together and reinforcing a sense of place that says, "This is where you belong." Strips malls don't do this; real downtowns do. To begin the process of building places as opposed to projects, a community needs to look at their best opportunity. Is it a place like High Line Park—where trees growing up through abandoned tracks say "park" to two locals? Does an abandoned hospital or school allow you to create a new community center or build something very new—like a joint police and community center in Milliken, Colorado? How can you use your streets to reinforce place? Each community needs to identify what opportunities they have available, choose their best chance at success, and then energize it through robust community engagement. This creates the hand and toe holds needed to climb up and to the next great place—not project. In doing this, we build social capital, we build places for shopping, for playing, for local art work, for jobs, for community gardens, and for people to come, relax, and enjoy their achievement as a community.

Michigan's state motto is *Si Quaeris Peninsulam Amoenam Circumspice* / If you seek a pleasant peninsula, look about you. I have been looking around Michigan for fifteen years. Natural Michigan is stunning and diverse, and it sustains the state's top industries of agriculture, tourism, and timber. Given such abundance, it is easy to linger on the magnificence of this Great Lakes state and to give the built environment passing consideration. If we are to improve the health and quality of life for residents and visitors, and build sustainable, vibrant communities, we must turn our attention to improving the built environment by providing quality places that bring us together. We should measure our success not in miles of travel, but in the smiles associated with travel.

Dan Burden, executive director and co-founder of The Walkable and Livable Communities Institute, is an internationally recognized authority on livable and sustainable communities, healthy streets, traffic calming, and bicycle and pedestrian programs. Burden has more than 35 years of experience in creating livable communities with a focus on active transportation. He served for 16 years as the first state bicycle and pedestrian coordinator in the United States with the Florida Department of Transportation (1980-1996)—this program became a model for other statewide programs. Burden has worked with 3,000 communities to improve the built environment. Learn more at www.walklive.org.

Making room for all users, East Lansing, Michigan. Courtesy of www.pedbikeimages.org - Dan Burden

detroit: the democratic city

PHILLIP COOLEY

I moved to Detroit in 2002 with aspirations to follow American art critic, poet, and educator Peter Schjeldahl's advice on how to become an artist; "You move to a city. You hang out in bars. You form a gang, turn it into a scene, and turn that into a movement." Six years prior, I had been living in Chicago, Milan, Paris, New York, London, Tokyo, and Barcelona as a film student and a male model. The travel and experiences were wonderful, but it was time for me to add substance to my life. It was time to pick a city where I could find like-minded people and make an impact.

I had just finished reading a collection of essays, "Air Guitar" by Dave Hickey, which helped me reconsider the city that intrigued me the most—Detroit. It is the greatest American city in which to make art. It's affordable, inspiring, collaborative, and encouraging. The infrastructure seems to be a perfect fit as well—plenty of space and incredible access to industrial equipment. So I left the glamorous life of male modeling, night trains, and one-star hotels, and moved to Detroit.

Growing up in a rural city north of Detroit, I often visited the city for its inspiring art, music, and cuisine, but I never fully understood it. I knew that I did not always perform well while playing by the rules or waiting in line. I needed a place that would allow me to experiment and make mistakes. Detroit is not lawless in the sense that you can walk up to anyone on the street and commit a crime and expect to get away with it. Instead, laws are loosely followed when they restrict us, versus allowing us to progress responsibly. For example, many people keep bees in the city because it is necessary for our ecology and the honey is delicious. This is an illegal practice, but an example of a law that should not be followed. There is less red tape and bureaucracy here because we have more important things to worry about.

Café D'Mongo's Speakeasy, Detroit, Michigan. Courtesy of Marvin Shaouni

THE PATH TO ENTREPRENEURIALISM

The next step in my Peter Schjeldahl journey was to hang out in bars; I thrived at that. I was so fond of bars that I worked in them as well. I bar backed at The Buddah Bar on 8 Mile and I was the janitor at The Lager House in Corktown. When I asked the owners of The Lager House whether I should vacuum or sweep the floor because the worn carpet had become more of a dirt floor than anything else, they just laughed. It is still my favorite job to this day. I took great pride in putting ice in the urinals and caring for one of the dirtiest places in the city. It was a combination rock 'n' roll/motorcycle bar, and as history has taught us, those things do not always go well together. For example, one night, a punk decided to use the patio as a toilet, inches away from a biker's girlfriend. Seconds later the punk's face had been busted open. The punk's friends were scaling the patio walls seeking revenge. Others and I created a human wall in order to protect the punks from themselves. One of those helping me was Brian Perrone. Brian was selling burritos on the patio and working on a rock 'n' roll variety show called, "Hot Plate" where he would cook at musicians' houses while they had live shows. Brian was taking a break from the fine dining world, but he was still passionate about food and Detroit. After long discussions about the culinary arts, we decided to open a restaurant together. Dean St. Souver, one of the owners at The Buddah Lounge, would join us. Dean had a ton of experience in the design/build field and his bar was tanking. Brian then picked up a fourth partner, Michael Metevia. While they perfected the recipes, Dean and I designed and built the restaurant. Two years and many doubts later, we opened Slows Bar B Q. I originally moved here to become a musician or a filmmaker, but I ended up dropping out of a master's in architecture program and opened a restaurant instead.

It is often said that Detroit is a blank canvas. This expression can be interpreted as insensitive to the history of Detroit and all of the great work that has been accomplished in the past forty years. However, I agree with this statement in the sense that we are in a unique position to correct the mistakes that we have made and avoid the mistakes of others. Detroit has the opportunity to become the first major American city to be socially just, environmentally conscious, and fiscally sound. We are at a point in our history where we can avoid the traditional path towards gentrification, which leads to displacement, complacency, and homogenization. Others around the world are watching—they see Detroit as an amplified version of their current and future struggles and as a possible solution or lesson learned. By no means do I wish to discredit or forget the tremendous work that has been done nor ignore the disturbing historical facts that caused our decline such as the destruction of the neighborhoods of Poletown and Black Bottom, but I do not wish to limit Detroit's possibilities for recovery. I feel that this is our chance to right wrongs and correct our course. It is too late for many cities. They will go through the hardships that we have. However, we have the opportunity to not only lift our great city up, but also provide a map for others that are either going through many of the same struggles or will in the future. We must look to examples from our own neighborhoods as well as from those across the globe.

The author's restaurant, Slows Bar B.Q., Detroit, Michigan. Courtesy of the Michigan Municipal League

GRASSROOTS ART

The Happy Planet Index, an innovative index that measures the well-being of people in the nations of the world while taking into account their environmental efficiency, rates Costa Rica as the happiest nation in the world. However, the International Monetary Fund ranks it 84th based on GDP. Costa Ricans live longer than Americans and report higher levels of life satisfaction, while they only use up a quarter of the resources that we do. Costa Rica decommissioned its military in 1949, and used the money instead for education. As we continue through this global recession, we are learning that we all must do more with less.

In the Santa Marta favela of Rio de Janeiro—favela refers to shanty towns in Brazil—Dre Urhahn and Jeroen Koolhaas, creators of community-driven art intervention, used the power of color and line to inspire a neighborhood. They worked with unemployed youth to paint much of the favela. They hoped that it would draw comparisons to the famous statue of Christ over the city, but instead of being a gift from the government to the city, "it is a gift from the favela to the city." Urhahn recently described the favela to *Ode Magazine* as "a source of inspiration and creativity and thinks it's a shame they are maligned by the nations wealthier set, which dance to the music created there." They used their creativity and inexpensive paint to show the potential of people and combat misconceptions about violence and crime.

Resourcefulness is nothing new to Detroit. If actual unemployment hit 40 to 50 percent in most parts of the nation, there would be great civil unrest. Detroit has lived for years with high unemployment averages and continues to be culturally relevant. Detroit is also a wonderful example of the fact that wealth does not lead to happiness. Every warm, sunny day on Belle Isle, which was designed by Frederick Law Olmsted, thousands of Detroiters are out barbecuing, exercising, and checking out the cultural sites. Rich and poor come together and forget about the challenges we face to celebrate our great strengths as a community. Eminem, Kid Rock, Derrick May, Adult, The White Stripes, J-Dilla, The Dirtbombs, The Detroit Cobras, and many other tremendous artists did not come from a place of privilege, but instead from a sincere place that greatly affected their professional lives. These are just the musicians that were playing around town when I moved to Detroit. Motown—with too many musicians to mention—Iggy Pop & the Stooges, The MC5, and Bob Seger all changed the history of music. These musicians were all created from a place of necessity. The sincerity of their work is apparent and the shoestring budget that most started on, inspiring.

The Heidelberg Project, Detroit, Michigan. Courtesy of the Michigan Municipal League

ENTREPRENEURS ARE PART OF THE COMMUNITY

In many cities, opening a similar business would be viewed as competition, but in Detroit you are generally greeted with open arms and welcomed as a neighbor. We work together and share resources while realizing that there is enough for everyone and we are stronger in numbers working together. Experiences are often shared and there are few secrets. Entrepreneurs find the low barrier of entry helpful, as well. It allows you to learn and grow with your business at a more natural, organic pace. There is such a strong need for so many things in Detroit that fulfilling that niche is possible and makes owning a business all that more rewarding. You are not just an entrepreneur in Detroit; you are part of a community.

Le Petit Zinc is a quaint and friendly French restaurant in Detroit's oldest neighborhood, Corktown. The owners opened without the budget for an architect or general contractor. The community came together and drafted their architectural plan and pulled their permits in order to make up the budgetary gap. We also built them dining room tables out of reclaimed lumber. The restaurant is a tremendous asset to the community and all who helped on the project have recouped their costs over and over again in non-traditional ways such as through press coverage, raised property values, and quality of life improvements.

Two successful entrepreneurs, Claire Nelson and Liz Blondy, started Open City, a forum for aspiring and current business owners to exchange ideas and information about doing business in the city. As residents, they were frustrated by the lack of small businesses in the city. This support group for aspiring entrepreneurs could potentially ease their path to opening and then running a business in Detroit.

Artists Kate Daughdrill and Jessica Hernandez started a micro-fund event called Detroit Soup. Everyone pays five dollars to vote for a project from several presented that evening. The project that gets the most votes receives the money. This not only funds a project, but also builds community and encourages dialogue. Others throughout the city have followed this same method of micro-funding while acting as catalysts for many projects, big and small.

Entrepreneur and T-shirt designer, Philip Lauri. Courtesy of Kath Usitalo

SOCIAL ENTREPRENEURIALISM

Detroit has a rich history of social activism. This is how we will combat the traditional paths of gentrification. We will grow together as a socially responsible city, not only because of the watchful eye of the activist community, but also more importantly, because the city demands it. In choosing to live and work in Detroit, you choose to participate. It is next to impossible not to get involved in or be affected by your community.

Eric Howard is the executive director of Youth Nation. Eric noticed that many of the children in his southwest Detroit neighborhood were getting involved with gangs because of the youth's attraction to "low riders," (a style of car originated by Chicano communities that sit lower to the ground than most other car styles), culture, and graffiti art. He did not take away the things that they were passionate about, but rather, he removed the negative aspects of the art forms and focused on the positive, developmental roles in which graffiti and low riders can play. The youth are currently working with Detroit Collaborative Design Center to clean up an alley, some abandoned lots, and homes. They are creating a graffiti gallery that will invite the community into a once frightening space. During this process, I spoke to a bright young man who worked tirelessly on the gallery. He let me know that he would be attending College of Creative Studies (CCS) in Detroit the following year and studying fine art.

This past summer, Piquette Place, a $23 million apartment facility with 150 one-bedroom apartments, opened its doors to homeless veterans. Services at the facility include mental health counseling, substance-abuse treatment, job training, computer labs, and educational programs to help the veterans develop self-sufficiency and reintegrate into the community. Coalition on Temporary Shelter (COTS) programs—emergency shelter, transitional housing, and permanent supportive housing—are designed to address individuals' needs and circumstances and support them in moving along a continuum from homelessness to housing and stability. Two licensed child care centers provide quality care for the children of COTS' shelter guests and transitional housing residents so that they can work, seek housing or employment, attend school, or take other steps to rebuild their lives.

Veronika Scott, a junior at College for Creative Studies, designed a jacket that captures the user's body heat during the day to use at night when it doubles as a sleeping bag. The formerly homeless at Cass Community Social Services were taught industrial sewing skills in order to manufacture the jackets. Veronika stated, "It is designed to become obsolete. I am not advocating living on the street. I want it to do more than just keep them warm, but to also teach these people new skills so they can feel a sense of pride and know that they are capable of putting their skills to work to gain employment and provide a better life for themselves." The members at Cass Community Social Services also manufacture rubber doormats out of recycled tires that have been dumped illegally throughout the city. Veronika, Cass Community Social Services, COTS, and many others are coming up with innovative solutions to help the approximately 18,000 homeless men and women in Detroit.

Architectural Salvage Warehouse Detroit (ASWD) is a non-profit that deconstructs structures as opposed to demolishing them. Deconstruction recycles or reuses approximately 95 percent of the waste generated from taking down a structure, while demolition only recycles approximately 25 percent. Construction and demolition waste make up 26 percent of our waste stream in the U.S. Deconstruction diverts 18 percent of our waste stream while providing jobs five to one over demolition. Deconstruction is a wonderful way to learn construction. ASWD hires early release prisoners, a group of people that are often discriminated against when looking for employment.

TURNING LIABILITIES INTO ASSETS

The landscape of Detroit is one that demands engagement. Innovative public spaces are creating community—forcing residents to openly converse and work together. The environment is ripe for reconsideration. A collapsing home can be perceived as a natural resource if you look at it through the eyes of ASWD. An abandoned factory can be reactivated as a space for creation and production or turned into public space that records our industrial past. Abandoned land can be used to grow food in a city where some residents do not have proper access to fresh and healthy food. The possibilities are endless, and more and more people are turning liabilities into assets.

When Tyree Guyton became fed up with the drugs and crime on Heidelberg Street in the east side neighborhood that he grew up in, he did not complain about it. He showed the world that hard work and passion overcome any obstacle, regardless of size. He turned his neighborhood into a public work of art, which people from around the world have come to experience, and drugs and crime were forced out. Guyton did not build the Heidelberg Project with a million dollar budget. He built it with found objects, free and discounted paint, and a tremendous amount of hard work.

Design 99 is an organization that creates everything from bathroom tile designs to neighborhood planning strategies. An architectural designer, Gina Reichert, and her husband, artist Mitch Cope, are the duo behind Design 99. They set up shop to offer design services for 99 cents a minute or $99 per house call. They turned a foreclosed house into what they call the Power House which serves as a hands-on demonstration center for sustainable design. It runs on solar power and wind energy and will eventually power other homes in the neighborhood. "Design is a combination of public service, problem solving, and creative ideas," Reichert says.

Their work has not only inspired artists from all over the world to live and work in Detroit, but also more importantly, it has given hope and activated many of their neighbors. Corine Vermeulen-Smith, photographer, bought a foreclosed house on the north side of Detroit near Mitch and Gina of Design 99. She turned the house into a photography studio and shot free portraits of community members. In her own words, "Stemming from a desire to introduce ourselves and get to know the residents of a particular neighborhood, we solicited people to come into the studio via flyers, posters, and a fair amount of courting on the streets." In five days she recorded 85 beautiful portraits.

Chazz Miller started Public Art Workz in the northwest neighborhood of Brightmoor. He says, "Our purpose is to foster social and emotional growth while educating students that art is in everything and should be used to achieve their highest academic performance and a mastery of skills necessary to become effective and productive members of society." Realizing that he could not change the city without changing the hearts and minds of the people, Chazz set out to bring people together and inspire them to work together, get a job, or just pick up trash. As Chazz states, "it's not about Chazz, it's about the community."

Greg Holm moved to New York after living in Detroit for years. When he came back to do the Ice House project—freezing an abandoned house to reference the urban conditions in the city and beyond —he was hesitant to undertake the project, due to fear of exploiting the community. That hesitation forced him to engage the community and open up dialogue about his work. Holm communicated with the neighbors of the project, in the hopes of inspiring the local community and potentially some future artists. He also fed people soup throughout the cold winter in order to give back to the city that was supporting him. The project became so much more than a beautiful photograph and social critique; the city and environment, which made the project possible in the first place, pushed Holm to become a more conscious artist.

When the city of Detroit determined that it no longer had the budget to operate Clark Park in southwest Detroit, citizens came together and refused to allow it to be closed. They took over programming and operations while the city agreed to mow and provide lights. It is now bustling with youth soccer, baseball, tennis, hockey, and many other programs. It would have joined the numerous ranks of abandoned land, had citizens not stood up and taken responsibility for such an incredible asset. Another city park, Roosevelt Park, lies in the shadow of the historically brilliant and infamously abandoned Michigan Central Station. Members of the community reached out to others for program ideas after Daimler Financial generously offered to bring 60 volunteers and $20,000 to do a project in the park. Each year, the budget, number of volunteers, and their impact have grown. Following the city's master plan, community members have started to plan and design phases of the park based on community needs. The plan is to remain flexible and organic in order to adapt to the changing needs of the community. Over $600,000 of private dollars and in-kind donations have been dedicated to the park with more coming in.

The description of Detroit as a food desert is sensationalist and inaccurate. We are fortunate to have no chain grocery stores, but instead we have amazing localized grocery stores where the owner actually acts according to his suggestion box. Honey Bee now carries organic eggs after the customers asked for them. The eggs come from Michigan and are under three dollars a dozen. We do have many neighborhoods that need a grocery store—not big chain grocers. Instead, we need more independent grocers owned by Detroiters. Urban agriculture has rapidly grown in the fertile environment of Detroit. The massive amounts of abandoned land, coupled with the need for access to fresh produce, has spurred a type of innovation rooted in the earlier days of our beginnings. We have quickly become a world leader in this growing movement.

efore: Roosevelt Park with the train station in the background.

After: A group of citizens took matters into their own hands.

A future vision of Roosevelt Park. Architecture drawings courtesy of uRbanDetail and Todd Heidgerken

THE GREENING OF DETROIT

Greening of Detroit (a nonprofit founded in 1989) has not only done a terrific job of replacing some of the millions of trees we've lost to Dutch elm disease and the emerald ash borer, but has also developed many tremendous urban agriculture programs, partnering with the city, residents, and other non-profits.

As described on their website, the story of Shar Foundation and Recovery Park is "a narrative about how a collaborative effort can lead to neighborhood economic recovery through projects like urban farming. The narrative shows how urban farming can impact the local economy through job creation and neighborhood improvements. Jobs are created directly through urban farming activities and many more jobs are created in downstream activities such as food processing, packaging, and logistics." Shar is ready to plant this spring, pending some simple zoning variations already in progress. A 30-acre farm will provide 10 to 12 living wage jobs and will be matched with 2 to 3 times that in processing, packaging, etc. Michigan State University's Group for Sustainable Food Systems estimates that Detroit can grow 75 percent of its needed vegetables and 40 percent of its fruit on 2,000 acres.

Greg Willerer, founder of Brother Nature Produce, did not ask permission of the absentee landowners around his home to farm on their land—he asked his neighbors instead. His farm is now over an acre and feeds not only restaurants and customers at the Eastern Market, but also those in need. His farm is not fenced in. Woven into the fabric of the community, it is a gathering place for neighbors and even foreign travelers alike.

OUR VISION

Detroit's potential is limitless. We are in the fortunate position to change our course. New York and many other cities have become ships that are too big to steer. In Detroit, our infrastructure can continue to be a liability or we can choose to reassess our conditions and turn them into assets. We are a city that designs, engineers, and builds things. We have the technology and equipment to be relevant in a broader, more sustainable future. Until Michigan has a strong urban core, the state will continue to lose population, especially young talent. Detroit is the key to our state's recovery. Even though we have the upper hand, we must not make the same mistakes that the suburban population made when they left. We must work together or continue to decline.

Phillip Cooley is a part owner of Slows Bar B Q and a general contractor with O'Connor Development. He serves on the board of Architectural Salvage Warehouse Detroit, Greening of Detroit, Roosevelt Park Conservancy, Center for Community Based Enterprise, and The Heidelberg Project. Cooley is also on the advisory board of ACLU of Southeastern Michigan and currently co-chairs the Mayor's Advisory Task Force for the DetroitWorks project. "I'm fortunate to have a successful business and tremendous partners and staff. This allows me to be in the community as a volunteer, helping to design and build public spaces, helping others start small businesses, and working towards creating a just and sustainable Detroit." Cooley lives in Detroit.

place management: society's missing level of governance

CHRISTOPHER LEINBERGER

Developed societies and their economies are very complex animals. They are far more complicated than in the industrial era a half century ago or agricultural societies 200 years ago. The layering of the knowledge economy on top of both the industrial and the agricultural economies is part of the reason for this complexity. The sheer size of countries and political entities such as the United States (309 million people in 2010), the European Union (501 million), India (1,150 million), and China (1,330 million) dwarf the leading nations and empires from 50 and 200 years earlier.

Expecting early 19th century or even mid-20th century governance structures to handle the challenges of the early 21st century is not realistic.

The governance of developed societies today includes many elements such as defense, diplomacy, energy policy, and economic policy that dominate the front pages of our newspapers and homepages of websites. Yet most day-to-day life is dominated by issues much closer to home, particularly how to build and manage the built environment. Issues of transportation options and congestion, zoning, land use, cleanliness of streets, and personal safety dominate the metro sections of our newspapers and countless websites—not to mention the hundreds of thousands of neighborhood organizations.

League Public Policy Forum, Detroit, Michigan. Courtesy of the Michigan Municipal League

The built environment, along with the real estate and the infrastructure that supports it, represents over 35 percent of the asset base of developed economies such as the U.S.; it is, in fact, the largest asset class in the economy. If one took the capitalized asset values of the New York Stock Exchange and the NASDAQ and doubled them, the built environment would be larger. This is why two of the past three recessions, including the so-called "Great Recession" of 2008-2009, were initially caused by the collapse of a major component of the built environment, housing. Subsequent economic expansions were significantly propelled by the investment in infrastructure and the recovery of real estate.

Another reason the governance of society is so much more complex today is that there are now two broad ways to build the built environment. During the agricultural era, cities were built as walkable urban places.[1] Transportation options included horses and water-borne craft, but the vast majority of people got around on foot. This meant that agricultural communities had to have a mix of different uses—housing, offices, craftsmen's workplace, retail, lodging—all within walkable proximity. Since a walkable distance is generally considered to be between half a kilometer (about a quarter mile) to a kilometer (about a half mile), that means these cities were between 120 to 640 acres. As a point of comparison, a typical regional mall including its parking lot is around 80 to 120 acres.

Drivable sub-urban development[2] is the second broad means of developing the built environment. It has been the basis of the built environment beginning in the 1920s, but especially since the late 1940s when it became the market-preferred method of development in the U.S. and, eventually, most of the developed world. In the U.S., encouraging drivable sub-urban development has been and continues to be the goal of domestic policy at the federal, state, and local levels of government. To the present day, it is the only legal way of developing real estate in the vast majority of jurisdictions throughout the U.S. But drivable sub-urban development has recently become overbuilt; the demand is substantially satisfied for possibly the next generation. In fact, overbuilding of drivable sub-urban development was the major catalyst of the Great Recession of the late 2000s. The crash and bailout of the development world's financial institutions by their governments was basically the bailout of drivable sub-urban development, particularly on the metropolitan fringe.

Starting in the mid-1990s, the market began to demand more walkable urban development.

---

1 Walkable urban places use multiple transportation options to get there, but once there, the preferred and most conventional method of getting around is walking. This puts a limit on how big these places can be since there is a limit on how far we want to walk. They are urban in so far as there are multiple uses (residential, retail, work places, hospitality, entertainment, restaurants, cultural, government, sports, parks, etc.) all within walking distance. Walkable urban places can be in the central city or the suburbs, so they should not be confused as only a central city phenomenon.

2 Drivable sub-urban development uses only cars or trucks for nearly all transportation to and within these areas. Walking is only an option for recreation since few meaningful places would be within walking distance or convenient or safe to walk to. These areas are sub-urban in so far as all uses are segregated from one another. There are residential-only areas, retail-only areas and workplace-only areas, all connected by roads and freeways. Drivable sub-urban areas can be in the central city or the suburbs, so they should not be confused as a suburbs-only phenomenon.

Aerial view of crowding & density, USA. Courtesy of www.pedbikeimages.org - Dan Burden

In most metropolitan areas, there will be many more walkable urban places built over the next generation than exist today.[3]

Yet creating and managing walkable urbanism is far more complex, risky, and unknown than conventional, drivable sub-urban development for those responsible for its development and management: government officials, design and legal professionals, the construction industry, real estate developers, and investors. American zoning, finance, and the skills and experience of real estate developers, as well as massive public and private subsidies, all encourage and even mandate drivable sub-urban development in most of the U.S.

Walkable urban development has pent up market demand that will take most of the next generation to satisfy.

Walkable urban development occurs in specific places, not randomly wherever a freeway or major arterial happens to roam. It is focused on a discrete, relatively small parcel of land that is governed by the natural limitations of how far humans are willing to walk. Much of the future demand for walkable urbanism will be met in central cities and inner suburbs, which means in-fill and brownfield redevelopment, a substantial challenge to make happen due to historic patterns of land ownership. Walkable urban places have many moving parts, and a minimum of those parts must be in place and smoothly operating together for the place to achieve critical mass; in other words there must be a "there, there." There must be an innovative strategy and aggressive management to make these places successful.

The crafting and implementation of the strategic management for walkable urban places is far more complicated than the largest regional mall, theme park, or commercial business park ever built. The management of walkable urbanism brings together private sector real estate developers and property owners, public sector elected and appointed officials, and the non-profit sector and surrounding neighborhood representatives. Proper management includes assuming responsibility for a variety of services that were publicly provided, including infrastructure investment, land assemblage and development, and perhaps most importantly, branding the place as unique, authentic, and transformative. It is about creating a "could-only-be-here" place.

As a result of this complexity, walkable urban places require a missing level of governance that does not now exist in society. It is important to note that this has not been phrased as a "missing level of government." Citizens of the U.S., in particular, feel there is too much government already. It is a level of governance "below" most city, county, township, and town governments, which is closer to the ground and comprised of a land area closer to the size of an agricultural-era town or city, as referenced above. This governance could be, and currently is, provided by the private sector, non-profit organizations, the public sector, or some combination of all three.

3 For further understanding of the pent-up demand for walkable urban development, go to *The Option of Urbanism; Investing in a New American Dream*, Island Press, 2008.

The Cherry Festival creates a sense of place, Traverse City, Michigan. Courtesy of the Michigan Municipal League

There are tricky legal and democratic issues involved with inserting a level of governance into the public realm. The U.S. Constitution was predicated on the states ceding power to the federal government. In addition, the states granted power to subsidiary political levels such as counties, cities, and towns. The concept of "states' rights" is usually thought of as a power struggle between the federal government and the states, but there is every bit as much controversy between the states and the levels of government closest to the people. Inserting yet another level of governance below the counties, cities, and towns is challenging.[4] The issues raised include:

> Who elects the governing board(s) of the organization or organizations?
> How are these organizations to be funded?
> Who benefits?
> How are risks shared?
> Who has to give up the power that they have today?
> How are the poorer citizens represented and enabled to live and work there affordably?
> How do existing government agencies work together with this new governance level?

This governance level managing walkable urban places is required because economic forces demand it, and current government structures generally do not provide for it. The federal partnership between Housing and Urban Development, Department of Transportation and Environmental Protection Agency in the Obama administration is demanding a more in-depth understanding of this phenomenon, as well as performance metrics to measure performance of these transformative places. The Office of Budget and Management is now evaluating agency budgets using "place-based" criteria.

The built environment has been responsible for many, if not most, economic downturns, but it is also a catalytic driver of economic recoveries. Few economic recoveries are healthy and create sufficient jobs without the 35 percent of the asset base tied up in the built environment being engaged in economic recovery. Since the market is demanding a different form of development—like walkable urban—which takes a fundamentally different and more comprehensive type of management to prosper, an economically sustainable recovery from the Great Recession and future recessions requires place management. The building of drivable sub-urban areas helped propel the U.S. and other developed economies in the 1950s through the 1990s. The building of walkable urban places—both revitalizing our center cities and transforming the suburbs—will be a foundation under economic growth for the next generation.

---

4 There is the need for another level of governance that does not exist in an adequate manner; metropolitan governance. First conceptualized by Jane Jacobs in her *Cities and the Wealth of Nations; Principles of Economic Life* (Vintage, NY 1984) and given much more justification by the Metropolitan Policy Program of the Brookings Institution, it is generally understood that metropolitan regions are the fundamental building block of the national economy. This level of governance is in-between the states and the counties, cities, and towns. There are numerous public, non-profit, and private entities that manage a piece of most metropolitan areas (in the United States, examples include metropolitan planning organizations, regional chambers of commerce, regional economic development organizations, council of governments, power companies serving the entire metropolitan area, etc.). The metropolitan strategy and management will be the subject of a future book.

The Detroit Riverwalk, Michigan. Courtesy of Downtown Detroit Partnership

THE 20TH CENTURY AMERICAN DREAM

The form the built environment takes is intimately linked to the underlying economic system. It is a by-product of, and also reinforces, the creation of wealth resulting from that underlying economic system. This connection between the general economy and the form of the built environment has been evident throughout recorded history. It has also been the basis of how the "American Dream," or any other economy's goal of the good life, has been visualized and built on the ground.

There have been two structural shifts in how the built environment has been built in the past hundred years. One took place in the early to middle 20th century, and we are in the middle of the second today. The first was caused by the shift from the agricultural economy to the industrial economy. The second is occurring due to the shift from the industrial economy to the knowledge economy that emerged at the end of the 20th century and early 21st century. Both forced the means of building the built environment from one extreme to the other—from walkable urban in the early 20th century to drivable sub-urban in the middle and late 20th century, and then back to walkable urban, that is occurring now.

Drivable sub-urban was a completely new way of building, never-before-seen in the 6,000 years of building cities and metropolitan areas. As families in the U.S. "saw the USA in their Chevrolet," driving to a drivable sub-urban house, shopping center, school or office, made the household wealthier. The linkage between economic wealth creation and the emerging drivable sub-urban communities was not just logical; the building of the suburbs helped grow the overall economy during the various booms of the 1950s through the 1990s.

When the U.S. began the drivable sub-urban experiment, we could only see the benefits. Leaving behind the dirty, noisy, crowded city for the Jeffersonian ideal of your own land and individual means of transportation seemed to have no downside. Besides, following the "birds-of-a-feather-stay-together" approach to society,[5] *they* had the notion that we could get away from *them*. What was there not to like? Focus group-validated Hollywood provided us with aspirational imagery in the popular television shows of the area, like *Leave it to Beaver, Dick Van Dyke*, and *The Brady Bunch*—all set in the beguiling suburbs.

Only through experience did we come to understand that the drivable sub-urban future was not entirely what it was cracked up to be. As more and more drivable sub-urban development took place, the very qualities households moved there for, such as open space, ease of getting around by car, and clean air, were destroyed. The operating principle of being drivable sub-urban is now understood to be "more is less." As more is built, the quality of life declines.

---

5 Miller McPherson, Lynn Smith-Lovin, and James M Cook, "Birds of a Feather: Homophily in Social Networks," *Annual Review of Sociology*, Vol. 27: 415-444 (Volume publication date August 2001), DOI: 10.1146/annurev.soc.27.1.415. http://www.annualreviews.org/doi/abs/10.1146/annurev.soc.27.1.415?journalCode=soc

Freeways for a car-centric culture. Courtesy of www.istockphoto.com/AlbanyPictures

THE 21ST CENTURY AMERICAN DREAM

The current shift from the industrial economy to the knowledge economy, which started in the late 20th century, has had profound effects on developed societies. The technological changes in everyday life, the need for computer literacy, the explosion of the service industries, and the growth of new products that have little or no variable cost of production—e.g., software, electronically delivered entertainment/information, video games, etc.—mean that a well-educated and continuously educated workforce is essential to household and national economic well-being.

With a new economy comes a new way of building the built environment. It is no longer necessary to encourage the purchase of cars to grow the economy, nor to mold the built environment around using cars for nearly every trip from home. For much of the past 60 years, nearly every metropolitan area only offered slight variations on drivable sub-urban housing and commercial space for those households that had options of where and how to live. An upper-middle class family in the late 20th century U.S. could either have a single family home close to a 1980s strip mall or one near a 1990s strip mall. There was basically no choice. If your household did not have a choice in the industrial era of how and where to live, which included many minority households and the poorer economic classes, you could either have the hand-me-down walkable urban neighborhoods built in the late 19th and early 20th century or a long commute to the opposite side of the metropolitan area where all the new and relocating jobs went.

The knowledge economy is now demanding choice in how and where to live—either drivable sub-urban or walkable urban—depending on time of life, family configuration, and preference. And the option of walkable urban should be in the suburbs as well as the central city. A particular household may want walkable urban excitement when young, and then later move to a drivable sub-urban place to raise the children, only to return to a walkable urban location after the children have flown the coop. Others may stay in walkable urban locations their entire adult life or do the opposite—live a drivable sub-urban existence, though occasionally going to walkable urban places for entertainment or culture. The knowledge economy demands choice.

The issue in the early 21st century is that nearly all metropolitan areas in the developed world do not offer nearly enough walkable urban alternatives. The built environment has far too many drivable sub-urban places to live and work, particularly in the U.S. where overbuilding the drivable sub-urban fringe was the ultimate catalyst for the housing meltdown, the mortgage crisis, and the multi-trillion dollar bailouts in 2008 and 2009.

Signs that many households want walkable urban homes and commercial life abound. They are easiest to see in the Hollywood offerings that the millennial generation aspired to while growing up. These television shows, which include *Seinfeld, Friends,* and, of course, *Sex and the City,* featured safe, exciting, and fulfilling walkable urban settings. In the shows, cars were only occasionally used for transportation—generally only for visiting their baby boomer parents still living in the suburbs. Most got around by transit or on foot.

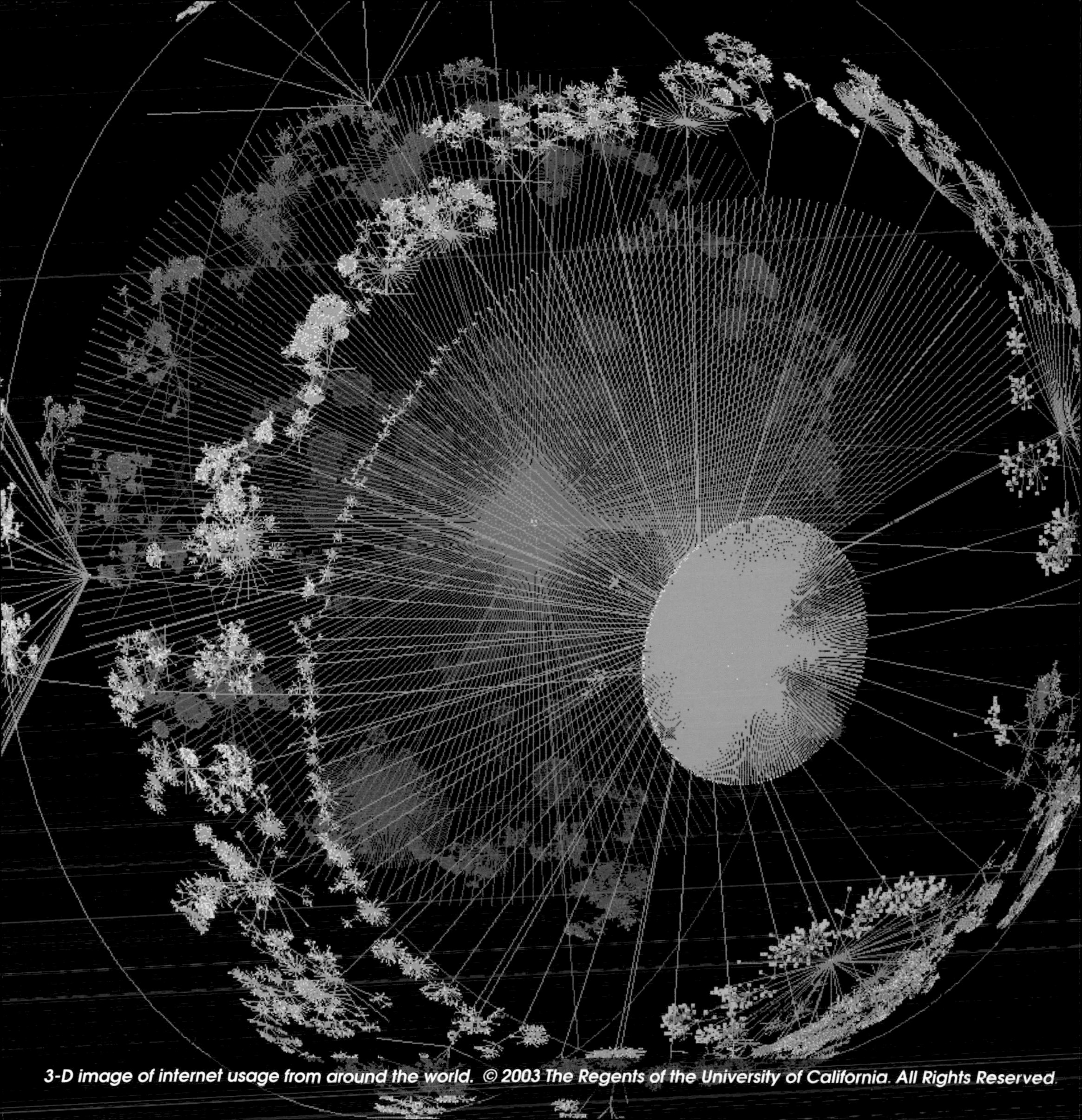

3-D image of internet usage from around the world.

The sure sign that walkable urbanism has significant pent-up demand is the price premium now associated with it. Walkable urban housing and commercial space get a 40 to 200 percent price premium on a price per square foot basis. Households pay 40 percent more to three times more for each square foot of living space in a walkable urban location than a comparable drivable sub-urban house. The most expensive housing in nearly all U.S. metropolitan areas in 2000 was in prestigious suburbs with one to 10 acre lots and nationally outstanding schools. By 2010, in many metropolitan areas, the most expensive housing was in the walkable urban districts of the central city and the inner suburbs on postage stamp-sized lots, many times with some of the worst school systems in the country. The lines crossed in the decade, reflecting the structural shift in what the market wants. The last time the lines crossed was probably in the 1950s and 1960s, going the opposite direction, reflecting the previous structure shift toward drivable sub-urban development.

It is estimated that on top of existing supply, an additional 20 to 40 percent of all households, depending on the metropolitan area, want walkable urban living and workplaces, assuming they could afford it. Given that only 2 percent is added to the built environment in good years, this means it will take at least a generation to satisfy that demand.

Building the walkable urban housing and commercial space that the market is demanding means an entirely new way of building infrastructure, beginning with transportation. This is because transportation drives development; the transportation system a society builds dictates where the rest of the infrastructure—water and sewer, telecommunications, primary and secondary education, public safety—goes and the type of real estate that is developed. Build only roads and you get drivable sub-urbanism. Build a mix of different modes, including rail and bus transit, biking, walking, and roads, and you can get walkable urbanism.

THE MAJOR UNINTENDED CONSEQUENCE OF THE WALKABLE URBAN FUTURE

There is no such thing as untroubled bliss. The same applies to the walkable urban future being built today and for the next generation. The leading unintended consequence is affordability. Right now, walkable urban places that are at "critical mass,"—i.e., the elements that make the place vital are mostly developed and operating, including transportation options, employment concentration, entertainment, supermarket, and safe streets—are the domain of the well-to-do. Only emerging walkable urban places that "urban pioneers" are creating are reasonably affordable. But if these pioneers are successful, these places will probably obtain the similar price premiums that the "critical mass" walkable urban places have achieved. The best visualization of this process is the 2001 *New Yorker* cartoon, to the right.

In many walkable urban neighborhoods, like Georgetown in Washington D.C., SoHo in New York, and Lincoln Park in Chicago, the 2010 caption could be "It was an artist's loft, then a lawyer's loft, and now it's an investment banker's loft."

"It was an artist's loft. Now it's a lawyer's loft."

The term for this phenomenon is, of course, gentrification which is either the most loved or most hated word in the walkable urban universe. The term is loved because over cocktails some people revel in how a place is being gentrified, resulting in increased safety, quality of life, restaurant options and, most importantly, one's housing investment going up. These same people may attend a public hearing where activists decry gentrification and subsequent displacement of existing residents as rents rise. While many of the long-term residents who own their own property are generally pleased to see their homes go up in value, which provides them with an unexpected boost in retirement savings, most public outcry is about displacement of renters.

The concern is legitimate and it is a major public issue. It requires a conscious affordable and workforce housing strategy over the next generation as more market-rate supply is built that will help reduce the walkable urban price premium. Increased supply is the major answer to the shortage of affordable and work force housing, but the supply shortage will take at least 30 years to get into some semblance of balance.

INTENTION, STRATEGY & MANAGEMENT

The need for place management has sparked a new level of governance throughout the developed world. Generally taking the form of business improvement districts (BIDs) in North America, these are nonprofits sanctioned by state and local government to perform various roles in a prescribed area, usually between 50 to 400 acres.[1] BIDs are generally financed by private sector property owners and they often take the form of a voluntarily imposed increase in property taxes that is dedicated to funding the annual budget.

Most BIDs start when the private sector determines that the status quo regarding the cleanliness, safety, festivals, the infrastructure, park management, and other aspects of the built environment are not adequately being maintained, and in fact, may not be addressed at all. The public sector may provide services such as safety and cleanliness, but the property owners decide it is not at a high enough level for what the market is demanding. In other words, the private sector has determined that the status quo must change and they have the intention to change it.

Built upon this intention to change, a strategic plan is usually developed that outlines the issues that most urgently need addressing, generally starting with "clean and safe" issues in the early years. A permanent organization is established, and then paid for by the voluntary taxes that property owners agree to raise upon themselves and their tenants.

The exciting aspect of place management is that it is evolving rapidly from its initial incarnation of a cost center, meaning that the BID provides services for an agreed upon annual budget. Today, many BIDs are becoming profit centers, allowing the organization to engage in activities that generate a profit from the activity. These can include managing parking, parks, and festivals, and providing private plaza management to private property owners. The profit can then be reinvested in the operations of the BID.

---

1 Note that the typical land area of a BID is about the same as a town or city in the agricultural era mentioned above.

Yet another level of place management is investment center activities. This involves raising substantial capital for investment in transit systems, parking decks, rebuilding parks, restaurants, and kiosks within parks, and even acting as a catalytic development firm. A catalytic development firm can acquire or put under control land, and it can engage in land development and joint venturing with private developers for vertical development.

Place management is becoming one of the most exciting new fields in real estate and the built environment. It merges private sector real estate development and public sector service provision with civic sector vision for the social good of the entire place and its many stakeholders. The experience of the past generation is but a fraction of what can be achieved in the future as place management assumes a major role in how we manage society. It does not come without controversy, as you would expect of a responsibility that is so complex and brings together so many different players, but ultimately, it creates "a there, there."

Christopher Leinberger, a land use strategist, teacher, developer, researcher and author, balances business realities with social and environmental issues. He is a professor and founding director of the Graduate Real Estate Development Program at the University of Michigan; visiting fellow at the Brookings Institution in Washington, DC., founding partner of Arcadia Land Company, a new urbanism, transit-oriented development and consulting firm, and president of Locus, Responsible Real Estate Developers and Investors.

Leinberger is the author of The Option of Urbanism, Investing in a New American Dream, *as well as the* Strategic Planning for Real Estate Companies. *He has written for numerous publications, such as the* Atlantic Monthly *and* Urban Land *magazine. He has been profiled by CNN, National Public Radio, Infrastructurist, the* Washington Post, *and numerous other broadcast, web, and print media.*

In 2009, Leinberger was voted one of the "Top 100 Urban Thinkers" in a poll conducted by Planetizen, the international urban planning and architecture website.

---

placemaking and resilient communities

DR. JOE VANDERMEULEN

Independence Rock is a long, rounded granite dome on a wide plateau in central Wyoming. Standing on this 130-foot high craggy rock outcrop, you can see the meandering Sweetwater River extending many miles to the west and the ruts left by thousands of wagon wheels along the old Oregon Trail leading off into Big Sky Country. Looking down at your feet, you can still see the names, inscriptions, and dates chiseled into the weathered rock by thousands of immigrants as they made their way west during the great migrations of the mid-1800s.

The story goes that migrants heading to Oregon and California by wagon train needed to get to this point by July 4th if they hoped to get over the Sierra Nevada Mountains before the winter snows. According to some reports, a number of entrepreneurs greeted the travelers and offered to help them chisel their names and messages into the famous rock—for a price. Today, Independence Rock is part of a Wyoming State Historic Site along Route 220, festooned with plaques and prominently advertised as an important stop for tourists.

Independence Rock was imbued with personal meaning by migrants and incorporated as an important political place in Wyoming's historic record. Though little more than a weathered granite outcrop, it gave travelers a vantage point, high ground along a seemingly endless desert expanse. From that prominence, the migrants saw hopeful changes ahead—grasslands, a river, and the long-expected mountains. This combination of narrative and emotional attachment is at the heart of how place is created. The eminent geographer Yi-Fu Tuan wrote, "From the security and stability of place we are aware of the openness, freedom, and threat of space, and vice versa. Furthermore, if we think of space as that which allows movement, then place is pause; each pause in movement makes it possible for location to be transformed into place" (Tuan, 1977, 6).

Independence Rock, Wyoming. Courtesy of Wandering in Wellington Blog

INTRODUCTION

The walls of my office building are plastered with maps of familiar places and dozens of photographs taken by the residents of many different Michigan communities. Some of the pictures look professional, most do not; but they are all beautiful. The pictures were taken by ordinary people specifically trying to capture their own sense of place—a family playing on a sandy beach near the pier in Grand Haven; people window-shopping on a downtown street in the village of Milford; and laughing school children, one splashing, one twirling, and one sitting in a large puddle along a cornfield near Adrian. The people pictured are interacting with specific cultural and natural features of their communities, making memories, and building a sense of place. Seeing, framing, and taking the picture also contributed to each photographer's sense of place. It was, in fact, an intentional placemaking activity.

This chapter reflects on 18 years of work with residents of Michigan communities, helping them develop a shared sense of place while taking steps toward greater sustainability and resilience. Admittedly, my work with communities as a journalist, hydrogeologist, and planner reaches back farther than that, but this chapter draws most on experiences in community planning and development work with the Land Information Access Association (LIAA).

When LIAA was created as a nonprofit community service organization in 1993, our first concern was with the diminishing amount of civic engagement and a growing distrust of local government. New processes and mechanisms were needed to support effective public involvement, including more inclusive community discussions, not just hearings, greater access to basic information—e.g., zoning ordinances and maps—and a greater sense of ownership and responsibility. Since that time, LIAA has partnered with the Michigan Municipal League (the League) and other statewide organizations on a wide range of efforts to design, demonstrate, and evaluate options for involving the public in community-asset mapping, cultural and natural resource development, and inclusive planning processes.

In 1995, the League and The Nature Conservancy partnered with LIAA on a unique research and demonstration project to develop a process for community development and discovery called Building a Sense of Place. Using emerging technologies of geographic information systems (GIS) and touch-screen kiosks—the web was not in use yet—LIAA engaged citizens and the local leaders from the cities, townships, and villages of seven different communities in processes to map and document the cultural and natural assets of those communities. The work focused on identifying what was valued and honored—the positive and potential of each community. Together, participants discovered that a sense of place develops as we deepen our knowledge of the cultural and natural resources of the community. We build a sense of place by learning about the area's history, cultural arts, commerce, public institutions, service organizations, and natural landscapes.

Montage of Farmington, Michigan. Courtesy of the City of Farmington

Mackinac Bridge. Courtesy of MML.

Manistee Lighthouse, Michigan. Courtesy of the Michigan Municipal League

These projects were the first efforts in Michigan to build multijurisdictional, community asset databases for direct public access. The participating residents, as well as public officials from adjacent jurisdictions, exchanged information and a growing understanding of what was most important about their shared communities. They also compiled base map data—e.g., parcels, planning districts, zoning—and formed new interpersonal and intergovernmental relationships. The seeds for cooperative planning and community development were planted in that shared sense of place.

Today, community and regional asset mapping is a part of a suite of web-based tools designed and used by LIAA and other organizations to help citizens and various interest groups gather and integrate information about place and place-based resources. These tools give local officials greater capacity to ask the crowd for advice, information, and direction such as crowd sourcing as well as providing for interaction with others such as through social media connections. Public information sharing and participation tools like these are extremely powerful in community planning and placemaking, and can be used to encourage and inform visitors. However, without interjurisdictional cooperation and effective public participation processes, their value is greatly diminished.

A FEW COMMENTS ON THE MEANING OF PLACE

Our conceptions of place and placemaking are not new. Nearly a century ago, the famous Scottish biologist and municipal planner Patrick Geddes called on local leaders, planners, and social activists to recognize that our cities are part of a greater whole; each place has a true personality that can be discovered by planners and others who love the place. In fact, Geddes may have issued the first formal call for regional asset mapping and documentation as a placemaking activity in his 1915 book, *Cities in Evolution:* "Hence our plea for a full and thorough survey of country and town, village and city, as preparatory to all town planning and city design..." (Geddes, 1915).

The power of place in the development and change of human communities is dramatic. As used here, place is a combination of the physical geography—e.g., location, landscape, human design—and the intangible values of human connections, including historical experience, community narratives, and interpersonal relationships.

The people who call a place home, if given a little time, may develop a sense of pride, emotional connection, and responsibility for the settlement or city. This informed attachment or sense of place is a key motivation when people make voluntary contributions to the cultural life of a community, work to resolve social issues, or participate in local government processes. In fact, civic engagement is at once motivated by and contributing to a sense of place.

Music in the park, Sault Ste. Marie, Michigan. Courtesy of the Sault Ste. Marie Conference and Visitors Bureau

In recent times, the meaning, value, and character of the places in which we live have been hotly debated. The booming growth of suburbs and exurbs from the 1950s until the collapse of the economy in 2008 has generated widespread concern over the inefficient use of resources and excessive land consumption.

Critics decried the inefficient, sprawling, and disconnected character of automobile-based suburban developments, calling them ill-defined, wasteful, community killers, which breed human disassociation and segregation (e.g., Jacobs, 1961; Jackson, 1985; Kunstler, 1993; Langdon, 1994). Harvard researcher Robert Putnam documented the unraveling of social connections in our communities and the decline of civic engagement, relating these impacts to characteristics of suburban sprawl (Putnam, 2000). In 2001, three distinguished professors concluded that places were becoming more unequal as federal and state policies have biased metropolitan development in favor of economic segregation, concentrated urban poverty, and suburban sprawl (Dreier, et al., 2001). Unfortunately, Michigan has been a leader in the conversion of land to inefficient low-density, urban uses.

After Michigan's first *Land Use Inventory* was completed in 1978, a number of state-level studies documented the rapid conversion of land to urban uses, extensive low-density development, redundant infrastructure, and increasing land use conflicts (e.g., *Smyth*, 1995; Michigan *Land Use Leadership Council*, 2003). Unplanned, piecemeal, and incremental development was relentlessly consuming familiar landscapes, contributing to traffic congestion, increased tax burdens, and the loss of critical cultural and natural resources. These negative impacts of poorly planned and uncoordinated land use were partly attributed to a lack of cooperation between the municipalities that often divide Michigan communities into a series of jealously guarded, independent jurisdictions.

PLACE AND THE CHALLENGED ECONOMY

What has been called the global New Economy has not been good to Michigan. Unemployment is higher and average incomes are lower here than in most other states. As recently noted by the Michigan League for Human Services (MLHS), median household income fell nearly 10 percent below the national average by 2009, while the state's poverty rate climbed to 16.2 percent of the population (MLHS, December 2010).

The experts tell us that Michigan has been slow to react to changes in the global economy. The departure of manufacturing jobs from the state and the general decline of the U.S. automotive industry were evident many years ago. At the same time, the knowledge economy described by Peter Drucker and others in the 1960s and 1970s has been supercharged with computing power and worldwide, high bandwidth data connections. Today, we are experiencing the global, knowledge-driven, and entrepreneurial economy, famously described in Thomas Friedman's book, *The World Is Flat* (Friedman, 2005).

Urban farming, Detroit, Michigan. Courtesy of Bloomberg/Getty Images

Economic development experts tell us that the future prosperity of Michigan in this new economy depends on our ability to make a number of key changes in our communities, regions, and state. Some of these prescriptions involve investing in higher education, aligning the K-12 education system with the new global economy, and keeping kids in school longer (e.g., Charles Ballard, 2010). We are told that communities must attract and retain well-educated and talented people called knowledge workers (Richard Florida's *Creative Class*) while building a more entrepreneurial culture and supporting technical innovation (e.g., Lou Glazer, Michigan Future Inc.; MSU's Land Policy Institute, Michigan Prosperity Initiative).

ECONOMY AND PLACE: PRESCRIPTIONS FOR PLACEMAKING

Placemaking is a far-reaching term used by planners and architects for many years to describe efforts to plan, design, and manage highly desirable neighborhoods, communities, and regions using a holistic approach. Focusing on human perceptions and experiences of place, the work of placemaking engages the public in the thoughtful design and connectivity of public spaces, capitalizing on local assets, and promoting cultural and social priorities (e.g., Walljasper, 2007; Landry, 2007).

There are a number of organizations, programs, and projects that have offered standards and techniques to improve the quality of places in recent years, including the Congress for New Urbanism, the U.S. EPA's Smart Growth Network, and the Project for Public Spaces. Some of the most frequently recommended elements for quality places include mixed-use developments, walkable neighborhoods, a range of housing choices, open space and recreation options, interconnected compact urban forms, alternative forms of transportation, and a true or authentic sense of place. With an emphasis on attracting knowledge workers, MSU's Land Policy Institute recently added that quality places should be unique, interesting, authentic, linked to the surroundings, and offer centers of activity (Wyckoff, 2010).

In many circles, placemaking tops the list of activities that communities and regions can undertake to improve their economic potential. If we want our communities to succeed in the new economy, we must make them attractive to the young, the educated, and creative people. The knowledge workers and entrepreneurs that move to our communities will be our next economic engine.

Mixed-use development, SkyLofts Market Square, Royal Oak, Michigan. Courtesy of the Michigan Municipal League

CAUTIONARY NOTE ON PLACEMAKING

In some ways, this emphasis on placemaking as economic development looks like older economic development techniques designed to attract manufacturing firms or mega-malls. For example, one well-regarded planner writes that large-scale placemaking real estate projects could contribute to "economic activity and prosperity in the metropolitan area and/or region" (Wyckoff, 2010). Rather than competing with other regions and states for smokestacks or warehouses, this competition is for the next Larry Page (Google) or Mark Zuckerberg (Facebook). However, there appears to be little or no evidence that specific placemaking efforts lead to increased populations of knowledge workers and entrepreneurs. While we may be able to characterize the things in a community that are popular or describe the features present in an economically successful community, all we can say is a correlation exists.

To be sure, placemaking is an important part of building high-quality communities, but for what purpose? A municipality fixed on economic expansion and growth may not ask the question, "What will make this community as satisfying as possible?" We run the risk of investing in the specifications of an imagined person who might bring us fame and fortune through magical entrepreneurship. Rather than casting about for ideas from other cities and towns hoping to hook the creative class, communities will be more likely to succeed by honestly and inclusively engaging current residents in the ongoing visioning, planning, and action processes that are building the community with an authentic sense of place.

PLACE AND HOME ECONOMICS

Apparently, the global portability of capital means that our communities and regions must compete with others by building an educated workforce, encouraging entrepreneurial development, and developing or attracting an educated creative population. We are told that capital is necessary for the creation of wealth and, presumably, wealth is necessary for the creation of happiness. Economic development experts say that in the new economy, capital will select places to settle; we need that capital and the creative class to grow our local and regional economies.

From this perspective, the physical reality and social construct of place is only as meaningful as it is marketable. If we hope to see economic improvements in our communities, we must provide the physical comforts, cultural amenities, social engagement, support services, and simple conveniences desired by educated and youthful entrepreneurs. Then we need to market the place to them as something distinct or unique, an attractive idealized vision.

The Farmers Market, Ann Arbor, Michigan. Courtesy of the Michigan Municipal League

On the other hand, if the global climate is changing and energy costs are going up, communities have much more to worry about than projecting an image as attractive social settings. While politicians debate the causes of climate change and argue about responses, communities are feeling the impacts of unprecedented weather events. There is no debate about catastrophic windstorms, debilitating heat waves, or rainstorms that flood whole cities. Communities are vulnerable to the impacts of dramatic weather events and surging energy costs. And the global systems upon which we depend for food, tools, and commodities are also vulnerable.

We live in a time when adaptive change is required. We may seek economic development in the New Economy by attracting a larger quotient of educated, creative people, but that may be an inadequate response. Taking a more holistic approach, we may find that the real work is less about place as attraction, than place as resilient community.

We don't have to look far to see that some of earth's resources are limited and that the world's human population is pushing the limits. Clearly, the costs of accessing energy-dense fossil fuels are increasing dramatically, and there is mounting evidence that global production of oil has already peaked (e.g., see www.iea.org; the International Energy Agency). In short, everyone who uses oil and gasoline can count on paying much more for these products in the future. Christopher Steiner's book, *$20 Per Gallon*, does a nice job of summarizing some potential effects of increased gasoline prices. Rapidly increasing costs for such a primary energy resource will dramatically limit both the mobility and financial capacities of many community residents. This threat is made more complex by the challenges of global climate variations and extreme weather events.

The global climate is changing. Direct measurements have documented increases in average air and ocean temperatures, widespread melting of snow and ice, and rising sea levels (Intergovernmental Panel on Climate Change, 2007). For the Midwest, important climate implications include significant changes in temperature and precipitation—both averages and extremes—and increases in the intensity, frequency, and duration of extreme weather events such as heat waves, drought, floods, and storms of all kinds (National Research Council, 2010). Effective responses by communities and regions need to be more than expanded disaster management. Communities need the capacity to absorb shocks, make necessary changes, and carry on with essentially the same functions; that is, they need to become more resilient.

Overflow from the Mississippi River flooded a downtown district. Courtesy of Istockphoto.com/niknikon

PLACEMAKING AND RESILIENT COMMUNITIES

The functions of community planning and economic development are changing dramatically as local governments struggle with the ongoing recession and the impacts of the new global economy.

As described, there are a number of strongly encouraged placemaking activities that will improve the quality of our communities, potentially making them more attractive, engaging, and welcoming to knowledge workers and entrepreneurs. Many of those activities, when properly planned and executed, could also serve to increase community sustainability and resilience, but the emphasis needs to be on local capacities and local economy.

To increase community sustainability and resilience, we need to take a systems approach to economic development and local investments. We need to ask how local investments can increase our safety and security while contributing to a vibrant, culturally rich community with the social and aesthetic services we desire. These strategies would increase community capacities, reducing the risks posed by disruptions in food, energy, and commodity supplies.

In his carefully researched book, *The Small Mart Revolution* (2006), Michael Shuman encourages communities to use economic development strategies that increase local ownership and import substitution. Like other economic development specialists, he argues that the diversification in employers and local business is necessary. But in diversifying business, we should put a premium on local ownership. In addition to providing more jobs, locally owned businesses help to keep money in the community, offer tangible and near-home investment opportunities—not simply faceless mutual funds—and foster a culture of entrepreneurship and creativity. They can also increase local self-reliance. By focusing on local markets and import substitution, communities can reduce the amount of money leaking out to other parts of the world. Further, local production is decentralized and sized to meet demand, keeping inventories and transportation costs low.

Reducing oil and gas dependency is a primary motivator of the Transition Town Movement, a fast-growing international social movement that focuses on building resilient, diversified local economies that greatly reduce dependence on fossil fuels. Adherents are encouraging communities across the world to realign the production of goods and services within ecological limits, enhancing local economies through family-owned businesses, community cooperatives, and local investment strategies. Transition Town groups have already formed in several Michigan cities (www.transitionus.org and www.transitionnetwork.org).

The international association of local governments known as ICLEI – Local Governments for Sustainability provides technical consulting, training, and information services to support sustainable development at the local level—Grand Rapids and several other Michigan cities are members. A primary component of that work is focused on helping communities adapt to changes in climate, including the management of severe weather events. The strategies

Solar parking meter, Ann Arbor, Michigan. Courtesy of the Michigan Municipal League

they recommend for municipalities are focused on increasing community resilience and include: increasing energy efficiency and distributed power generation through multiple renewable sources; increased flood control with functional wetlands, healthy forests and open space; urban tree planting and other actions to reduce heat-island impacts; improved building standards for greater wind and flood resistance; and diversified water supplies with conservation and rainwater harvesting efforts (www.icleiusa.org).

Building community resilience and placemaking are, in fact, overlapping forms of economic development. In working toward increased diversity and density in urban environments with improved transit options, and walkable mixed-use developments, we are working toward greater energy efficiency and less dependence on fossil fuels. But we need to look beyond urban forms, to address other critical factors such as food system security and distributed energy production.

Building community resilience and placemaking are, in fact, overlapping forms of economic development.

For example, we can increase community-wide food security by increasing both local production and consumption while building a popular slow food/local food restaurant scene. There may always be imported food, but local food systems can reduce a community's vulnerability to supply disruptions while enhancing the local economy—e.g., growers, food processors. For many Michigan communities, improving food security may require increased cooperation between adjacent jurisdictions for farmland preservation as well as investments by the community in new farm start-ups or processing facilities.

CONCLUSIONS

Over the years, I have had the pleasure of working with hundreds of dedicated, smart, and creative local government officials. Most are well aware of the central role they play in helping citizens articulate their sense of place and a common vision for the future of their communities. However, they tend to understate their capacity to convene community discussions and facilitate local planning and development processes. Too often, elected and appointed local leaders fail to recognize opportunities to engage citizens in forums for learning and respectful discussions. As a result, some of the most important challenges facing our communities are not acknowledged. Civic engagement turns into citizen action and efforts to skirt the deliberative and democratic processes established in Michigan law. In fact, respected organizations such as the Project for Public Spaces have encouraged citizens to do it on their own (Walljasper, 2007); while the *Transition Town Handbook* encourages people to work around local government (Hopkins, 2008).

The threats of extreme weather events and big increases in gasoline prices are as real as the continuing recession. Our communities need to adapt. But the preparations and responses must be measured, realistic, equitable, and supported by the citizens. To achieve these ends, local governments need to demonstrate the capacity to plan realistically, invest wisely, and cooperate effectively across jurisdictional boundaries. The cities, townships, and villages that collectively compose Michigan communities, must look beyond their borders. If the local economy is to be improved, community food systems secured, and energy production diversified, local officials from adjacent jurisdictions must find common ground and engage the public in frequent, creative, and hopeful discussions.

There is little doubt that most of us would prefer to live in high quality, vibrant communities. However, we are at a point in human history when it's not just about finding nice places to live and work. We are also concerned that communities have the strategies and capacities to stay that way.

Given the changes and challenges that lie ahead, sustainable and resilient communities are certain to become increasingly attractive places for people and for economic development.

Dr. Joe VanderMeulen is the executive director of the Land Information Access Association (LIAA), a non-profit community service organization located in Traverse City. LIAA was formed 18 years ago to increase civic engagement in community development and resource management through professional planning practices and the application of advanced information technologies. Trained as a welder, VanderMeulen has been a sheet metal worker, a journalist, a hydrogeologist, and a science advisor to the Michigan Legislature (Science & Technology Division Director, Legislative Service Bureau). He holds a BA in English and creative writing as well as a BA and MS in earth science and hydrogeology from Western Michigan University. He received his PhD from the University of Michigan in Natural Resources and Environmental Policy winning the Ayers Brinser Award for his research in land-use policy and the applications of geographic information systems.

REFERENCES CITED

Ballard, Charles L. *Michigan's Economic Future: A New Look.* East Lansing: Michigan State University Press, 2010. Print.

Cresswell, Tim. *Place: A Short Introduction.* Malden, MA: Blackwell Publishing, 2004.

Dreier, Peter; John Mollenkopf, and Todd Swanstrom. *Place Matters: Metropolitics for the Twenty-First Century.* Lawrence: University of Kansas Press, 2001. Print.

Friedman, Thomas L. *The World is Flat: A Brief History of the Twenty-First Century.* New York: Farrar, Straus & Giroux, 2005. Print.

Geddes, Patrick. *Cities in Evolution.* London: Williams and Norgate, 1915. Web. 28 Dec. 2010.

Heifetz, Ronald, Alexander Grashow, and Marty Linsky. *The Practice of Adaptive Leadership: Tools and Tactics for Changing Your Organization and the World.* Boston: Harvard Business Press, 2009. Print.

Hopkins, Rob. *The Transition Town Handbook.* White River Junction, VT: Chelsea Green Publishers, 2008. Print.

International Panel on Climate Change (IPCC). *Climate Change 2007: Mitigation of Climate Change.* Metz, B., O.R. Davidson, P.R. Bosch, R. Dave, & L.A. Meyer, Editors. Cambridge, U.K.: Cambridge University Press, 2007. Print.

Jackson, Kenneth T. *Crabgrass Frontier: The Suburbanization of the United States.* New York: Oxford University Press, 1985. Print.

Jacobs, Jane. *The Death and Life of Great American Cities.* New York: Random House, 1961. Print.

Kunstler, James Howard. *The Geography of Nowhere.* New York: Touchstone, 1993. Print.

Landry, Charles. *The Art of City Making.* London: Earthscan, 2007. Print.

Langdon, Philip. *A Better Place to Live: Reshaping the American Suburb.* Amherst: University of Massachusetts Press, 1994. Print.

"Michigan's Land, Michigan's Future." Final Report of the Michigan Land Use Leadership Council, 2003. Web. 17 Dec. 2010.

Michigan League for Human Services. "Michigan's Economy Continues to Cause Pain: Communities of Color Take a Harder Hit." December 2010. Web. 31 Dec. 2010.

National Research Council's Panel on Adapting to the Impacts of Climate Change. "Summary: Adapting to the Impacts of Climate Change." Washington:National Academy of Sciences, 2010. Web. 1 Dec. 2010.

Putnam, Robert D. *Bowling Alone: The Collapse and Revival of American Community.* New York: Simon & Schuster, 2000. Print.

Shuman, Michael L. *The Small Mart Revolution: How Local Businesses Are Beating the Competition.* San Francisco: Berrett-Koehler Publishers, 2006. Print.

Smyth, Paul. *Patterns on the Land: Our Choices, Our Future.* Lansing, MI: Planning & Zoning Center, 1995. Print.

Steiner, Christopher. *$20 Per Gallon - How the Inevitable Rise in the Price of Gasoline Will Change Our Lives for the Better.* New York: Grand Central Publishing, 2009. Print.

Tuan, Yi-Fu. *Sense and Place: The Perspective of Experience.* Minneapolis: University of Minnesota Press, 1977. Print.

Walljasper, Jay. *The Great Neighborhood Book: A Do-it-Yourself Guide to Placemaking.* Gabriola Island, BC: New Society Publishers, 2007.

Wyckoff, Mark A. "Placemaking, Sense of Place and Place-Based Initiatives." Planning & Zoning News. v. 29; n.1 (November, 2010): 6-15. Print.

the role of "place" in economic gardening

ROB FOWLER & MARK CLEVEY

In its simplest terms, economic gardening is a grow-from-within economic development model. It is important to note that economic gardening is NOT small business development or simply traditional business retention and expansion.

In his first State of the State address, Governor Rick Snyder said, "We need to put more emphasis on economic gardening as opposed to hunting. For those unfamiliar with economic gardening, it means we will focus first and foremost on building businesses that are already located here in our state." In so doing, he laid out a new strategy for economic development in Michigan and challenged communities and economic development organizations to think differently about job creation.

At the Small Business Association of Michigan (SBAM) we began studying the issue of economic gardening in the fall of 2008. Since then, we have conducted research on second-stage companies—those that have grown past the startup stage but have not grown to maturity—studied best-practice in economic gardening across the country, conducted pilot projects working directly with second-stage firms, convened policy experts and entrepreneurs, and ultimately authored a policy document titled, "Blueprint for Propelling a New Economic Direction for Michigan." It is our belief that an entrepreneur-centered economic development strategy holds the best potential for economic revitalization and job creation in Michigan. Along the way we have also come to understand the importance of "place" in developing a comprehensive economic gardening strategy.

Done right, economic gardening is a hybrid retention/ expansion program that consciously applies business acceleration-related support resources and incentives to the innovative and entrepreneurial segment of the small businesses sector.

Entrepreneurialism contributing to a sense of place. Zingerman's, Ann Arbor, Michigan. Courtesy of the MML

ECONOMIC GARDENING AND SENSE OF PLACE

The word, "entrepreneur," derives from the French verb "entreprendre" (to undertake), and entered the English language in the 1400s in the form of "enterprise" (commonly used to refer to an undertaking of a bold and arduous nature)[1]. The person engaging in the enterprise was known as the "enterpriser." Both terms eventually gave way to "entrepreneur," the primary definition for one who organizes, manages, and assumes the risk of a business or enterprise. In more recent times the definition of entrepreneurship has come to mean one who "assumes the risks to transform ideas into sustainable enterprises that create value."[2]

There is significant evidence to show that entrepreneurs are the engine of the economy and have potential to catalyze economic recovery, diversification, and development in the state. Many have suggested that "economic gardening," a proven grow-from-within business model focused on high growth firms, can be effectively applied in Michigan to stimulate such entrepreneurial development. SBAM, along with the Michigan Municipal League, Michigan State Housing Development Authority, and others have suggested that "place" is an essential component of any effort aimed at generating economic revitalization through the accelerated formation and growth of innovative entrepreneurs. Moreover, SBAM's research suggests that economic gardening can be significantly enhanced when it is combined with sense of place to form a new combined community/economic development hybrid. It is this combination that engenders a robust community-level entrepreneurial culture, which, in turn, enables entrepreneurial ventures that successfully combine innovation with intent and capacity for growth to create jobs.

ECONOMIC GARDENING

Economic gardening is a nationally recognized reinvention model developed by Christian Gibbons, director of the Economic Gardening in Littleton, Colorado. In a paper released by the U.S. Small Business Administration, Office of Advocacy titled, "Look Ahead: Opportunities and Challenges for Entrepreneurship and Small Business Owners," economic gardening is highlighted as one of five "opportunities" for economic development and job creation.[3] Closer to home, Daniel P. Gilmartin, Michigan Municipal League Executive Director and CEO, also notes that today's global economy demands a different approach—growing knowledge-based jobs through "economic gardening and entrepreneurship."[4] Finally, economic gardening has been resoundingly endorsed by SBAM and Michigan's own Edward Lowe Foundation.

---

1 *The Oxford English Dictionary*: first use of the word "entrepreneur" appeared in the book *Nobility* in 1475.

2 Judith Cone, Kauffman Foundation

3 Moutray, Chad, Office of Advocacy, U.S. Small Business Administration, "Look Ahead: Opportunities and Challenges for Entrepreneurship and Small Business Owners," (October 2008), pp 8.

4 Daniel P Gilmartin, Executive Director & CEO, Michigan Municipal League, "A Community's Role in Entrepreneurship," in, *The Review* (official magazine of the Michigan Municipal League), November/December 2009, pp 4.

In its simplest terms, economic gardening is a grow-from-within economic development model. Most importantly, it should be noted that economic gardening is not small business development or simply traditional business retention and expansion. Done right, economic gardening is a hybrid retention/expansion program, separate and distinct from, but closely integrated with other business attractions and/or retention/expansion programs within a community, which consciously applies business acceleration-related support resources and incentives to the innovative and entrepreneurial segment of the small businesses sector. In discussing the Littleton program, the Edward Lowe Foundation notes,

"While it was introduced as a demonstration program to deal with the sudden erosion of economic conditions following the relocation of the largest employer in the city at that time, it has emerged as a prototype for a rapidly expanding movement of like-minded economic developers looking for additional methods to generate truly sustainable economic growth for their communities, regions, or states."

For Michigan's purposes, economic gardening raises three important community and economic development related questions:

(1) What types of businesses have the greatest potential to generate significant economic activity?

(2) As an economic revitalization strategy, should the public sector direct resources to firms that have potential for growth or treat all small businesses as equal?

(3) How can the accelerated formation and growth of homegrown entrepreneurial firms be best supported and incentivized?

With regard to the type of businesses that have the greatest potential, the Edward Lowe Foundation, for example, has found that both firm age and size are key drivers of job creation, and most net new job creation is generated by firms that are one to five years old; these firms create more net new jobs than their older counterparts, as well as a higher average number of jobs per firm. Generally, firms that fall within this category are second-stage businesses. The Edward Lowe Foundation has shown that businesses can actually be grouped into stages, each with a different set of associated risks—e.g., challenges and opportunities such as technology, market, market growth rate, management and manufacturability. Second-stage businesses—firms with 10 to 99 workers with revenues between $1-$50 million—are one of the most important contributors to a dynamic entrepreneurial economy.

... an entrepreneurial culture is a necessary condition for robust small business entrepreneurship.

Most importantly, not all firms that meet the size definitions of second-stage companies are innovative and entrepreneurial. The true potential of those second-stage firms that do effectively combine innovation with intent and capacity for growth can be seen in a historical view of the annual "Michigan 50 Companies to Watch" program that celebrates second-stage companies throughout the state. Known for their performance in the marketplace and innovation, as well as sales and employment growth, these companies come from a wide range of industries across the state.

From 2006 to 2009, these companies generated $1.2 billion in revenue and added 629 employees, both in Michigan and out of state, reflecting a 71 percent increase in revenue and 64 percent increase in jobs for the four-year period. That translates into a 20 percent annual revenue growth and 18 percent annual growth in employees. These companies project continued growth in 2010, with a 22 percent revenue increase and 22 percent growth in employees in Michigan and out of state when compared to 2009. If their projections hold, these companies will have generated $1.6 billion in revenue and added 976 employees over the last five years—a 108 percent increase in revenue and 100 percent increase in jobs since 2006. That this occurred in spite of a very difficult Michigan economy makes it all the more impressive.

The question as to whether innovative entrepreneurship should be actively encouraged directly relates to its potential to have a dual positive impact on both communities and the economy. One of the key findings of SBAM's work is that an entrepreneurial culture is a necessary condition for robust small business entrepreneurship. SBAM finds that such an entrepreneurial culture must include, but goes well beyond, a business friendly environment. A community with an entrepreneurial culture is one that can benefit from the "social capital" associated with entrepreneurship.

Raymond W. Smilor, for example, author of *Entrepreneurship and Community Development*, notes that, "Entrepreneurship can also help confer identity, belonging, and security not only on those who elect to start and grow enterprises, but also on those who join them in that effort and on the wider environment in which they operate."

Google notes that an "(e)ntrepreneurialist culture is not just relevant to business and engineering students contemplating starting their own businesses. It is just as relevant to people who intend to seek employment with large companies or, indeed, are going to enter public service—non-governmental organizations, charities, museums, hospitals, universities, public school administration and the like."

Finally, Christian Gibbons notes that economic gardening is not just a business development effort, but also more of an integrated economic and community development. According to Gibbons, "Economic development and community development are two sides of the same coin. A community without many amenities is going to have a hard time being an environment for entrepreneurs—especially as their wealth starts to grow."

Because entrepreneurial culture is essential to robust entrepreneurship, the question of how best to encourage entrepreneurship directly relates to its potential for both community and economic revitalization. Through the Sense of Place Council—comprised of public and private sector members to improve the quality of places in Michigan—there is a growing school of thought that suggests intentional placemaking can contribute to economic vitality. Thus, any viable economic revitalization strategy must incorporate both community and economic development principles—sense of place—if it is to be successful. In the August 2010 Sense of Place Council Logic Model, the Council officially reported on the need for new policies and strategies to stimulate entrepreneurship in the state, including economic gardening.[5]

A community with an entrepreneurial culture is one that can effectively benefit from the "social capital" associated with entrepreneurship.

A "virtuous cycle" is a phenomenon where a greater number of innovative people leads to shared ideas which leads to growth in institutions that foster innovation, that in turn attract more innovative people from less fertile communities and so on.

---

5 Michigan State Housing Development Authority/Michigan Municipal League Sense of Place Council, Sense of Place Council Logic Model, August 2010.

SENSE OF PLACE: FRAMEWORK FOR A VIRTUOUS CYCLE

SBAM poses that innovative entrepreneurship can be effectively enhanced and enabled in Michigan by combining both community and economic revitalization with the context of sense of place. Our research suggests that it is the combination of economic gardening with sense of place that fosters entrepreneurial culture. It does so by creating conditions where a "virtuous cycle" can occur—where a greater number of innovative people leads to shared ideas, which leads to growth in institutions that foster innovation, and in turn attract more innovative people from less fertile communities, and so on.

...most net new job creation is generated by firms that are one to five years old (these firms create more net new jobs than their older counterparts, as well as a higher average number of jobs per firm).

An entrepreneurship-related virtuous cycle enables an entrepreneurial culture by fostering the formation and growth of innovative entrepreneurship in all sectors in three very distinct ways:

- ***Small Business Entrepreneurship – A small business entrepreneur is an individual that effectively uses the strategic management principles and practices of entrepreneurship to combine innovation with intent and capacity for growth in high growth potential markets and industries. One of the key benefits of entrepreneurship in Michigan is its potential for positive impacts on older workers. Duke University scholar Vivek Wadhwa found that older entrepreneurs have higher success rates. Indeed, the Kauffman Foundation reported that the highest rate of entrepreneurship in America has shifted to the 55 to 64 age group, with people over 55 almost twice as likely to found successful companies as those ages 20 to 34.***

- ***Intrapreneurship – An intrapreneur is an entrepreneur that operates within an existing host company or organization. The term "intrapreneurship" dates to a 1983 PhD dissertation (Burgelman) and was later defined in a 1985 book by Gifford Pinchot titled,*** **Intrapreneuring*****. According to Pinchot, "Intrapreneurs can make all the difference between your firm's success and failure." Most importantly, intrapreneurship can be an effective instrument to drive diversification.***[6]

---

6 For more information on how to rekindle intrapreneurship within an existing company, see: Brendan Boyle, *Creating an Entrepreneurial Culture of Optimism: Companies That Innovate Well Often Share a Positive Culture*, Jan. 14, 2008.

• Social Entre/Intrapreneurship – Serial entrepreneur Josh Linkner tells would-be entrepreneurs that "if you're going to be an entrepreneur, do it to make a difference. The social impact of entrepreneurship is its real value."[7] 1980, Bill Drayton, a management consultant working for McKinsey & Company, coined the term "social entrepreneur" as an individual who effectively uses entrepreneurship principally to make a difference by generating positive social change. Most importantly, social entrepreneurs operate in both the private and non-profit sectors, and thus are an essential and vital component of community and economic recovery, diversification, and development. As one of a handful of states that allow L3C Corporations—low-profit, limited liability corporations that are fast becoming the organizational structure of choice for social entrepreneurs—Michigan is well positioned to use social entrepreneurship to help bring about community and economic recovery, diversification, and development.[8]

ECONOMIC GARDENING MODELS

It is important to note that the policies, strategies, and initiatives characterized as "economic gardening" vary widely. They are experiments that differ in their content, scale, delivery systems, pricing strategies, and marketing approaches; this is not surprising for an innovation that only in recent years has moved beyond its roots in Littleton, Colorado. The field is still in a highly creative stage, which means that those conducting pilot tests or demonstrations are blazing the trails they are traveling.

Following the city of Littleton's example, the state of Florida and the University of Central Florida (UCF) have together launched a similar model of offering services to its second-stage businesses in six regions throughout the state to aid in their growth. Along with other services, UCF is offering information resources similar to those in Littleton, as well as decision making tools—e.g., strategy analysis and capital referrals. UCF develops the tools and distributes them to businesses via technical assistance teams that work in the six regions.[9]

Wyoming employs a strategy that includes the Wyoming Market Research Center, a statewide center for economic gardening tools. Wyoming offers a variety of tools to its small businesses at no cost. The most updated information available reports that the size of the economic gardening program has increased from serving 57 businesses in 2003

---

7 Josh Linkner, November 9, 2010 Keynote Speaker, MIT Enterprise Forum, Great Lakes Chapter, 2010-11 Savvy Entrepreneur Series.

8 The L3C is a low-profit limited liability company (LLC) that functions via a business modality that is a hybrid legal structure combining the financial advantages of the limited liability company, an LLC, with the social advantages of a non-profit entity. An L3C runs like a regular business and is profitable. However, unlike a for-profit business, the primary focus of the L3C is not to make money, but to achieve socially beneficial aims, with profit-making as a secondary goal.

9 GrowFL, "Cultivating Growth Companies" (2010) <http://www.growfl.com/>

to 286 businesses in 2007.[10] While it is true that Wyoming has implemented this program on the state level, it should be mentioned that it is still operating at a relatively small scale. Michigan has over 10 times as many firms as Wyoming, so a proportional program in our state would be serving more than 3,000 firms.

Georgia implemented a Littleton-like economic gardening model throughout many regions within the state. The model started out as many interrelated economic development programs and morphed into an economic gardening program. Georgia understood that it would be challenging to implement a small, regional program on a statewide level, so it set out very specific parameters of who the program was intended for and the goals of the program.[11]

MODELS IN MICHIGAN

Michigan has experimented widely with economic gardening and many of the most innovative economic gardening initiatives are occurring in our state. SBAM has identified five distinct models that use some variation of economic gardening tools and practices that are separate and distinct from conventional business retention/ expansion practices:

- Open-Source Model – Ann Arbor SPARK is a powerhouse for innovation-based business development in Washtenaw County and beyond. Ann Arbor SPARK also provides one of the most comprehensive service packages in the nation to area businesses through an "Open Source Economic Development" economic gardening model, based, in part, on principles developed by Edward Morrison, Purdue University.

- Rural Entrepreneurship Model – The Land Policy Institute at Michigan State University operates a rural entrepreneurship program called Creating Entrepreneurial Communities (CEC). The CEC project works with small community leadership teams, drawn from across Michigan, to learn about and execute tailored local approaches to encourage business start-ups and support entrepreneurs through all phases of business development. Another example of rural entrepreneurship is the Sirolli Institute Model of business development for communities experiencing severe economic stress.[12] The model creates a cadre of community specialists—its "facilitators"—that actively focus on the creation of new small businesses. It is anticipated that some of these new startups will grow and be the beneficiaries of traditional economic development incentives that will accelerate their growth and result in economic development in the community.

---

10 Economic Gardening Part Two (2009). <http://blog.edcsouthwestcalifornia.com/blogpost-15751/Economic-Gardening.html>

11 Steve Quello and Graham Toft, "The Small Business Economy for Data Year 2005: A Report to the President," U.S. Small Business Administration, Washington, D.C., Chapter 6, "Economic Gardening: Next Generation Applications for a Balanced Portfolio Approach to Economic Growth," December 2006, 157-193, <http://www.sba.gov/advo/research/sbe_06_ch06.pdf>.

12 See: Sirolli Institute, http://www.sirolli.com/Home/tabid/36/Default.aspx.

SBAM has identified five distinct models that use some variation of economic gardening tools and practices…

- Open-Source Model
- Rural Entrepreneurship Model
- Blended Model
- Economic Gardening Plus Model
- Regional Entrepreneurship Collaborative Model

The SPARK East Incubator, Ypsilanti, Michigan. Courtesy of the Michigan Municipal League

• Blended Model – Midland Tomorrow operates a blended economic gardening program, based on the Bakersfield, California model, that combines a traditional business attraction approach—"hunting"—with a strong business creation, retention, and expansion effort—"gardening" Under this model, a vibrant entrepreneurial culture is an essential part of the business attraction effort. The Keweenaw Economic Development Alliance (KEDA) in Houghton, Michigan, is Michigan's longest running example of a successful blended economic gardening in the state. KEDA was created by community leaders in 1969, and their efforts have significantly diversified the local economy, reduced its susceptibility to economic downturns, and helped foster the creation and growth of innovative entrepreneurial businesses.

• Economic Gardening PLUS (EGPlus)[13] – EGPlus poses that an entrepreneurship culture is one where three distinct types of entrepreneurs are prevalent: small business entrepreneurs; intrapreneurs; and, social entre/intrapreneurs (both non-profit and private sector). EGPlus is designed to foster a "virtuous cycle" within the context of a sense of place by providing Economic Gardening programs and services for all three types of entrepreneurs.

• Regional Entrepreneurship Collaborative Model – The Regional Entrepreneurship Collaborative (REC) is a new Great Lakes Bay Region based economic gardening program in Bay, Midland, and Saginaw Counties that is operated by Saginaw Valley State University. It builds upon a previous and highly successful program—Workforce Innovation in Regional Economic Development (WIRED) program operated by Saginaw Valley State University. The new REC initiative focuses on the mid-Michigan region and organizes entrepreneurial clients and related entrepreneur-support programs and services according to: a) venture stages; b) venture stage related risks; c) entrepreneur type—small business, intrapreneurs, social entre/intrapreneurs; and d) clusters—e.g., growth-oriented industry sector. This model provides regional economic gardening support services with a Council of Governments region. Individual communities identify, screen, and qualify candidate firms, and they coordinate the delivery of economic gardening related growth acceleration programs and services offered by the regional EG Service Provider (Shepherd Advisors, LLC).[14]

CONSIDERATIONS FOR AN ECONOMIC GARDENING STRATEGY IN MICHIGAN

Economic gardening is a significant "change in economic development philosophy, not merely adding new programs."[15] When operated within the context of sense of place, economic gardening becomes a significant

---

13 Economic Gardening PLUS is an approach developed by Mark H. Clevey, Co-Author, Michigan Entrepreneurship Score Card.

14 Shephard Advisors, LLC, 3820 Packard Road, #250, Ann Arbor, MI, 48108 - Initiated in 2000, Shepherd Advisors is a specialty management consulting firm whose mission is to "foster economic wealth and planetary health through the robust commercialization and deployment of clean technologies."

15 Jeffrey Padden, Blueprint for Propelling a New Economic Direction for Michigan, Public Policy Associates, Incorporated, 119 Pere Marquette Drive, Lansing, MI 48912. October 2010, pp iii.

change in community development philosophy as well. The economic gardening experience of Michigan and other states and communities suggests that Michigan has great flexibility in how we could design and implement an economic gardening program for the state. For example, economic gardening could be deployed through the current SmartZone system, through the regional Council of Government system, in individual communities as a MSHDA sense of place program, through the MEDC as a community development initiative, or in other ways. Moreover, economic gardening tool development could be supported from a variety of public and private sources.

Economic gardening is a significant "change in economic development philosophy, not merely adding new programs." When operated within the context of sense of place, economic gardening becomes a significant change in community development philosophy.

The core of the needed economic development change is to embrace economic gardening as an important addition to the state's current attraction, or "hunting" strategy. Economic gardening differs considerably from more conventional business attraction/retention economic development strategies as the following:

The Edward Lowe Foundation finds that Economic Gardening programs provide three distinct and important programs and services:

1. Information – Providing critical information needed by businesses to survive and thrive. Generally finds that second-stage entrepreneurial firms need strategic versus tactical market research.[16]

2. Connectivity – Developing and cultivating an infrastructure that goes beyond the basics and includes quality of life, a culture that embraces growth and change, and access to intellectual resources, including qualified and talented employees.

3. Infrastructure – Developing connections between businesses and the people and organizations that can help take them to the next level—e.g., business associations, universities, roundtable groups, service providers, and more.

Christian Gibbons has found that economic gardening is different from traditional business retention/expansion in that it:

- Targets firms that combine—or have the potential to combine—innovation with intent and capacity for growth and provides them with a specialized set of business acceleration incentives and resources.
- Builds on the experiences and insights of experts across the nation that are working at the cutting edge of public sector business development policies and practices.

---

16 Shepherd Advisors, Regional Entrepreneurial Collaborative: Regional Economic Gardening Working Session, December 9, 2010, Saginaw Valley State University.

• Relies more on providing knowledge and expertise to companies and less on providing tax dollars.

• Focuses on small companies that combine innovation with capacity and intent to grow.

SBAM finds that successful economic gardening programs also require a community development component if an entrepreneurial culture is to form and flourish. Towards that end, SBAM suggests that economic gardening be operated within a context of placemaking and that programs be designed to capitalize on the virtuous cycle associated with innovative entrepreneurship, intrapreneurship, and social entre/intrapreneurship.

• Emphasizes a market-based role for the public sector, rather than one that focuses principally on providing services.

• Assumes that business owners are smart enough to decide which services they are likely to find valuable and are willing to pay for.

• Acknowledges that the economic strategy to provide targeted support to skilled entrepreneurs is aligned with quality of life and placemaking strategies.[17]

Christian Gibbons, in his article titled "Economic Gardening," also suggests that there are several essential components of any successful economic gardening program:

The right people:

• High quality staff is the first and foremost. Staff should have a high level of skills in the technical areas of service including market research, web marketing, social media, etc., to help client companies grow in a variety of ways.

• The project director must be skilled at three scales: community politics, entrepreneurial, and economy. A project director must be competent at selling the economic gardening program, identifying with management of growth businesses and the community's political/business leadership, and understanding the economic environment.

Supportive Politics – Political support and political champions are key to long-term success. Long-term funding and support are vital, and communities need political leaders willing to go to bat for the program.

Design the program to succeed.

• Staff must have training in economic gardening principles. Economic gardening is not perfunctory business assistance; it is a multi-faceted process of providing dynamic growth support of highly variable businesses.

---

17 Jeffrey Padden, Blueprint for Propelling a New Economic Direction for Michigan, Public Policy Associates, Incorporated, 119 Pere Marquette Drive, Lansing, MI 48912. October 2010, pp 8.

- Use the full set of tools. Economic gardening relies upon a broad set of databases, skilled researchers, and a high-level corporate tool kit that includes Geographic Information System (GIS), social networking, web marketing, and management support and connection, among others.
- Implement at an appropriate scale. Generally, larger programs will have the scale of tools, skills, and companies that will enable the program to provide better service to more kinds of companies.
- Focus on second-stage companies. Most jobs are created not by the largest or the smallest companies, but by "Stage 2 companies, which are companies defined by having 10-99 Employees and $1M - $50M in annual sales."[18]

Christian Gibbons suggests that there are several essential components for any successful economic gardening program:

- *The right people*
- *Supportive politics*
- *Design the program to succeed.*

ECONOMIC GARDENING PLUS

In addition to the above, SBAM finds that successful economic gardening programs also require a community development component as well, if an entrepreneurial culture is to form and flourish. Towards that end, SBAM suggests that economic gardening be operated within a context of placemaking and that programs be designed to capitalize on the virtuous cycle associated with innovative entrepreneurship, intrapreneurship, and social entrepreneurship. Thus, the mentioned strategies and design components and features must not be limited to economic development and small business development specialists within a given community. It is critically important that community development, as well as business retention specialists and related stakeholders, be involved as equal partners in this new combined community/economic revitalization effort.

For example, the economic challenges facing Michigan are a double-edged sword for human services agencies. While the need for services is increasing, the financial resources to address such needs are dwindling. The United Way of Saginaw County offers social entrepreneurship training and funding to their agencies as a way to improve their capacity to produce positive social change in the community. In Detroit, Blight Busters unleashes and redeploys captured capital into new private-sector ventures such as the Motor City Java House.

Both Lawrence Technological University and Saginaw Valley State University offer intrapreneurship development initiatives designed specifically to help existing Michigan manufacturers rekindle their nascent entrepreneurship as a catalyst for business diversification. In other realms, private-sector intrapreneurs are actively incubating new innovative entrepreneurial ventures. For example:

18 Chris Gibbons, "Economic Gardening."

• DETROIT VENTURE PARTNERS – In the depths of the greatest economic crisis since the Great Depression, successful serial entrepreneurs Josh Linkner, Dan Gilbert, and others joined together to launch a new venture capital fund designed to "rebuild the region through entrepreneurship." In describing this new fund, Josh Linkner noted, "There is nothing more precious than entrepreneurship, innovation, and the Detroit region. Detroit rocks. Don't mess with the Big D".[19]

• DEVICE AND DIAGNOSTIC ACCELERATOR, LLC – Located in the Detroit suburb of Farmington Hills, Device and Diagnostic Accelerator, LLC has committed capital of $50 million for its client companies, and it will provide complete support to help entrepreneurs develop, test, and launch new medical devices. Device and Diagnostic Accelerator, LLC will cater to startups, second-stage companies, and those ready for the marketing stage. Client companies will be provided free rent, guidance in regulatory compliance, legal services, and business consulting in exchange for equity.

• MOMENTUM – Located in Grand Rapids, Momentum is a private-sector backed venture incubator that provides seed investments, intellectual capital, and mentorship to innovative web technology startups. Momentum is backed by a team of experienced entrepreneurs who act as mentors. The companies involved are business incubator Pomegranate Studios and the Winquest Group, an investment firm.

Education is America's longest running and most successful public-private partnership. Few would disagree with the notion that education is central to community and economic recovery, diversification, and development in Michigan. Within this context, while most colleges and universities across the state have embraced non-accredited entrepreneurial certificates, the University of Michigan has proposed a new joint master's degree in entrepreneurship through U of M's Engineering School.[20]

The proposed joint master's degree could finally end the insipid debate that has characterized the entrepreneurship education movement in Michigan over the last decade—whether or not entrepreneurship can be taught; whether entrepreneurship education has sufficient academic merit to warrant the involvement of major institutions of higher learning; or whether it is simply a course of study better suited to training. In one step, the University of Michigan has not only laid this debate to rest, but has significantly raised the bar for excellence in entrepreneurship education in the state.

---

19 Josh Linkner, 11/9/10, Keynote Speaker, MIT Enterprise Forum, Great Lakes Chapter, 2010-11 Savvy Entrepreneur Series.

20 For more information, please see: Aileen Huang-Saad, Ph.D., Assistant Director for Academic Programs, Center for Entrepreneurship, University of Michigan, 251 Chrysler Center, 2121 Bonisteel Boulevard, Ann Arbor, MI 48109. 734-615-7020 (office) 734-223-6059 (mobile) aileenhs@umich.edu

SUMMARY

Place is a vitally important element of any successful effort aimed at the generation of economic revitalization from innovative entrepreneurship. SBAM's work finds that an entrepreneurial culture is a necessary condition for the formation and increase of high-growth potential ventures. SBAM finds that such a culture is one where entrepreneurship is present in multiple sectors rather than being limited only to the small business sector. Most importantly, SBAM finds that having a sense of place is vitally important to entrepreneurial culture as it provides the catalyst for entrepreneurship to be applied in all sectors of a community.

Rob Fowler is the president and CEO of the Small Business Association of Michigan (SBAM). Formed in 1969 and with over 10,000 members, SBAM is the largest state-based organization in the U.S. focused specifically on the interests of small businesses. SBAM has been on the forefront of calling for public policies that support the creation and growth of innovative entrepreneurs in the state. SBAM's Foundation, the Small Business Foundation of Michigan, is the sponsor of the Annual Michigan Entrepreneurship Score Card (www.sbam.org). Fowler was a member of former Governor Granholm's Council of Economic Advisors and served as a member of Governor Snyder's Economic Development Transition Team.

Mark H. Clevey is a veteran of the United States Air Force, an honors college graduate, and holds a masters degree in public administration from Western Michigan University. He holds an advanced business counselor certificate from the Michigan SBDC and an economic gardening practitioners certificate from the Edward Lowe Foundation. Clevey has worked on behalf of entrepreneurship in Michigan for over 30 years in the private, educational and public sectors. Previously, he served as the executive director of SBAM's Foundation and SBAM's vice president for entrepreneurship. Clevey is currently the primary author of SBAM's Annual Michigan Entrepreneurship Score Card and SBAM's Economic Gardening and Entrepreneurship Consultant.

---

cultural economic development: an economic force waiting to be harnessed

DR. WILLIAM ANDERSON

Michigan's current economic reality shock has forced a new assumption. Thousands of manufacturing and supplier jobs tied to the auto industry have been eliminated. Recognizing that there are no economic development silver bullets, business and political leaders must find new ways to stimulate, diversify, and transform our state's economy. In 2006, Governor Jennifer Granholm said, "We are going to base our economy more and more on our intellectual property, on the creative side, the value-added side of what we can offer. The power of creativity in propelling our economy is a fundamental building block of our state's transformation."

Many experts have concluded that the world is shaping a new economy featuring a growing emphasis on technology, innovation, entrepreneurial thinking, and creative product development—what Richard Florida wrote about in his influential book, *The Creative Class* and Joseph Pine called *The Experience Economy.* This new economy, as so defined, bodes well for the future role of culture. In Michigan, we have defined cultural economic development as the process of using cultural resources to spur economic growth and community prosperity. Every community has cultural resources. The key is the ability and readiness to think and act strategically in the deployment of those cultural assets.

Traverse City Film Festival, Michigan. Courtesy of Traverse City

CREATIVE ECONOMY

The creative class represents a well-spring of entrepreneurial spirit, imagination, and originality resulting in real jobs that matter. The foundation of a creative economy is the capacity to attract and retain creative talent. A vibrant downtown, nightlife, a pedestrian-friendly community, walkability, affordable housing, and a place that welcomes diversity are prerequisites for the necessary environment. A place committed to incubate creative entrepreneurs is the overlay for a successful cultural economic development initiative.

As the following examples show, the importance of the creative economy is being taken seriously throughout the United States and around the globe.

According to a study sponsored by the Tourism Association of America (TAA), over

80%

of all adult travelers are interested in cultural/heritage experiences.

- "At a time of intense international competitiveness, arts and creativity will continue to play a significant part in injecting innovation and enterprise into the economy. . . The place of arts in creating living, vibrant communities is now widely understood."

  –Arts Council of England

- "Northern Ireland's creative industries have an important role in helping the UK become the world's creative hub. Creative industries in the UK are growing twice as fast as any other at the rate of 8 percent per year. Latest estimates suggest that Northern Ireland has around 2,500 creative enterprises employing 33,000 people or 4.7 percent of the workforce. . .As such the sector has a vital contribution to make and should not be viewed as being on the fringe, but as a central part of our economy. Creativity is all about new ideas, new products and services, new business sectors, new business models, and new types of business support."

  –Creative Minister David Hanson, MP Department of Culture, Arts and Leisure, United Kingdom, 2006

- "Wisconsin must intentionally, strategically, and collaboratively act to attract creative people to innovate products, services, and even business practices, or its attempts to benefit from the creative economy resources will remain unconnected, unminded, unpromoted."

  –Arts Wisconsin: Grow Wisconsin Creatively

- "The combined creative sector workforce in the Lansing (Michigan) metropolitan area constitutes a significant economic sector, over 9 percent of the workforce in 2006."

  –Art Works: Creative Invention/Reinvention: A Collaborative Cultural Economic Development Plan for Greater Lansing's Urban Center, 2009

Grand Rapids Art Museum, Grand Rapids, Michigan. Courtesy of Oscar Ramirez

CULTURAL ECONOMIC DEVELOPMENT: FRONT AND CENTER

The creative class represents a well-spring of entrepreneurial spirit, imagination, and originality resulting in real jobs that matter.

Cultural venues are usually located within the Central Business District (CBD) and can be rightfully considered anchor institutions—much like principal downtown retailers or anchor stores in a mall. Nearly all consultants and planners agree that a revitalization strategy must include methods of driving traffic into the downtown either because people live there or to motivate people to do business there. There are many examples of cultural venues attracting potential customers into the CBD. First, there is the construction of the new Broad Art Museum now underway on the campus of Michigan State University in East Lansing. The university could have elected to build this cultural institution in the heart of its campus, but instead chose a location along Grand River Avenue in the heart of downtown East Lansing which has, in the words of MSU President Lou Anna Simon, "two front doors." In addition, the city of East Lansing and a developer are planning to construct yet another cultural venue in the downtown—a theater.

“The Broad Art Museum and the Theater at City Center II will be cultural anchors for our downtown. They are located about five blocks apart on opposite sides of Grand River Avenue, on campus and one downtown. The downtown extends the entire five blocks and beyond in both directions. We believe that the location of these anchors will add significantly to the vibrancy and economy of our downtown. The two cultural destinations are close enough to one another to be considered part of one walkable pedestrian node, with elements such as restaurants, retail, and hotels to support the experience, but far enough apart to allow multiple smaller creative businesses to fill retail spaces in between the anchors and sustain a dynamic cultural district or corridor. It is also worthwhile to note that many people come to our city to visit the university without venturing into our downtown, and others are comfortable visiting the downtown but avoid campus. The placement of these cultural destinations is likely to break the invisible dividing line between town and gown and encourage visitors to experience our friendly college community as a whole.”

-East Lansing City Manager Ted Staton

The Detroit Symphony Orchestra, Detroit Institute of Arts, the Charles Wright African-American Museum, the Detroit Science Center, and the Michigan Opera Theatre are all big cultural anchors along Woodward Avenue in Detroit. The Michigan Opera Theatre, in particular, offers a strong illustration of the economic impact of a cultural anchor located in the heart of a city. The theatre, at 1526 Broadway—a short five or six block street—has attracted the development of several newer restaurants because of the audience attending theatre productions. In addition, the theatre needed patron parking so it purchased and renovated the weary old Hudson parking ramp which serves both its customers and others who come to this portion of reinvigorated mid-town Detroit.

In order to truly legitimize the cultural sector's role in economic development and convince decision makers, we must demonstrate the economic outcomes of job creation, capital investment, and contribution to the local tax base.

The same dynamic occurs in small town America where cultural anchors are located in the CBD. In Michigan, we have over 380 public libraries, a majority of which are located in the downtown area. Libraries are more than cultural magnets. They also often provide valued sources of information for the business community. Some have dedicated programs aimed at assisting business, such as the Spring Lake Library. It has a technology lab with up-to-date equipment that can be used for employee training. Currently, they use the space to train people wanting to start a business on eBay. The Portage District Library also offers business services, with dedicated staff, including one for "Starting & Running a Business."

CULTURAL ENTREPRENEURSHIP

If we believe that small businesses are a critical force in job development, and that one of the better strategic opportunities to accomplish that end is the attraction and nurturing of entrepreneurs, then the cultural sector represents a potential that is not fully being appreciated and tapped. Most economic developers focus on industrial growth as their top priority, recognizing that industries manufacture a product, which in turn creates wealth. Artists, too, create a product. A number of communities in Michigan have experienced success in developing live/work spaces for artists—the Dwelling Place in Grand Rapids and the Armory Arts project in Jackson are two prime examples. These enterprises create new businesses and jobs and often attract other development. In some cases, like the Dwelling Place on Division Avenue in Grand Rapids, they change the perception of place. The experience of Division Avenue in Grand Rapids with live/work spaces is instructive.

Formerly a prison, the Armory Arts Village is an engine for economic growth, Jackson, Michigan, Courtesy of the MML

“We discovered that artists generally were interested in this model because it allowed them to maintain lower costs when combining their residence and their work or studio space for one low cost. The presence of so many younger and creative types combined with major building renovations and public infrastructure improvements has caused a change in the public perception of the area. Many of these younger residents are also becoming engaged in neighborhood organizations and promotional activities leading to greater civic engagement with elected and appointed officials who have an impact on a wide variety of neighborhood issues. The reputation in this area for homelessness and hopelessness is gradually being replaced with an image of the area as ‘avante garde,’ which is often code for an artistically oriented area in transition. That change in perception has led to other investments, including market-rate apartments, restaurants, and other arts and entertainment-related venues. All of these changes have contributed to the local economy and are moving us closer to what some would characterize as the tipping point toward a fully revitalized, vibrant, and diverse neighborhood.”

-Dennis Sturtevant,
Director of the Dwelling Place

Much to their mutual credit, the cities of East Lansing and Lansing recently developed a joint cultural economic plan titled, "Art Works: Creative Inventive/Reinvention: A Collaborative Economic Development Plan for Greater Lansing's Urban Center." It proclaims a bold vision on page one: "This plan recommends that the cities of Lansing and East Lansing and the region be the Midwest's most welcoming and supportive destination for creative innovators and entrepreneurs." Though it is in the very early stage of implementation, Bob Trezise, Lansing's economic development director, is pleased with the immediate results. "The plan changed our entire dialogue. It gave a nearly invisible industry a new identity, a new credibility. The press and public bought into the months-long discussion about how there is economic value, in real numbers, to our arts and culture industry. It led to many editorials and other areas of public dialogue that suddenly produced an acceptance of the fact that the arts and culture community had real economic value that was measurable and worthy of being treated more seriously from a public and private standpoint. That set a tone that allowed for many other benefits to come upon the arts and culture community like new grants from municipalities, new incubator spaces for artists completed by the private sector, new loan programs, etc."

East Lansing's City Manager Ted Staton is on the same page. "We use a portion of our Community Development Block Grant allocation to assist individuals from low to moderate income households to start businesses through a program called the Cultural Entrepreneurship Program. It is jointly administered by the city of East Lansing and the Arts Council of Greater Lansing. The Grove Gallery Co-op in downtown East Lansing is essentially a privately operated incubator space that has individual studio space and shared gallery space for six artists. We have assisted three artists at the co-op through the Cultural Entrepreneurship Program." In its effort to attract artists, the city offers rent subsidies.

About a year ago, the four Michigan Main Street communities of Boyne City, Calumet, Niles, and Portland were selected to create cultural economic development plans. Niles, in addition, has its sights on attracting creative workers. Its plan calls for developing an environment that will attract creative entrepreneurs and then providing assistance to make their businesses successful.

CULTURAL TOURISM

Tourism is big business in Michigan. Based upon the data compilation of D.K. Shifflet & Associates, tourism had a $15.1 billion impact on Michigan's economy in 2009—of which $11.1 billion was generated by leisure travel. That financial activity produced nearly $1.2 billion in state tax revenue. We are good at selling our spectacular natural resources; they are the ace in our visitor marketing deck. Encouragingly, people are realizing that our diverse cultural attractions are another high card to play. Cultural tourism means providing the visitor with an engaging and memorable experience based upon our history, the real character of a place, culture, traditions, and creativity.

The market for cultural tourism is readily apparent. According to a study sponsored by the Tourism Association of America (TAA), over 80 percent of all adult travelers are interested in a cultural/heritage experience. With the current retirement of baby boomers, we have a population segment with more education and more disposable income than ever before. They represent a heaven-made market for cultural tourism. The age cohort 55-74 in North America is projected to increase by 35 million by 2025—another demographic that seems to be tailor-made for a cultural/heritage experience. The TAA study referenced here determined that cultural tourists spend more and stay longer than non-cultural tourists.

In order to be perceived as a destination, a place must have enough allure to motivate visitors to travel at least 50 miles for the express purpose of visiting a major cultural venue, community, or region, and cause them to stay at least two nights in the area. When that critical mass occurs, that party will have contributed to the local economy. When I think of major cultural venues in our state that may be considered destination attractions, there are three that come to mind—The Henry Ford Museum, the Detroit Institute of Arts, and Mackinac State Historic Parks (MSHP). Also, Michigan has two national heritage areas—the Keweenaw National Heritage Park and MotorCities National Heritage Area. Both are grounded in mega forces in our economic history of mining and automobile manufacturing. Mining was a dominant influence on the culture of the eastern upper peninsula. The residents of Houghton, Hancock, Calumet, and the Keweenaw Peninsula have recognized the visitor attraction of their mining history and are creating a unique visitor experience. On the other hand, in the southeast quadrant of the lower peninsula, the production of autos ruled the economy for many decades. If one were a pioneering leader living in Detroit with a plan to capitalize on this rich history, it would not have been unreasonable to conclude that the Motor City could fly solo in developing an automotive cultural tourism attraction. Yet in order to achieve greater critical mass for a common story, the MotorCities initiative involved a much larger circle of geography to include Lansing, Flint, and Saginaw—all of which have a major automotive heritage.

There are other themed cultural tourism regions in our state. Michigan has an exceptional maritime heritage featuring the longest coast line in the United States, except for Alaska; 120 lighthouses—more than any other state; one of fourteen national underwater sanctuaries at Thunder Bay; and many other maritime assets. The establishment of a National Marine Underwater Sanctuary at Alpena has served as an impetus for economic growth in this city and is surely destined to have an increasing economic impact. Mayor Carol Shafto is excited about the dynamic impact of this natural and cultural resource in her community. She states, "The Thunder Bay National Marine Sanctuary and Great Lakes Heritage Center not only preserves and protects a world-class collection of shipwrecks, but is a catalyst for cultural economic development in Alpena and the northeast Michigan region. Alpena is geographically isolated—75 miles at the nearest point from a freeway. You don't just 'happen upon' this community. The Thunder Bay National Marine Sanctuary is just that type of cultural magnet. From total obscurity at its designation in 2000, by 2010 the Marine Sanctuary program was serving 70,000 visitors a year, seven times the population of the city. The city of Alpena and its partners through Michigan Arts and Culture Northeast are seeking to make this community the center of cultural economic tourism for the region—to brand Alpena as the cultural hub for this part of the state of Michigan."

Thunder Bay National Marine Sanctuary, Alpena, Michigan. Courtesy of NOAA/Thunder Bay National Marine Sanctuary

REGIONAL DESTINATIONS: HERITAGE ROUTES

Developing a heritage trail or corridor is a common way to organize and manage a regional destination. The Michigan Department of Transportation has certified numerous Heritage Routes. Although there are a number of examples, three are particularly worthy of mention, given their ongoing state of development. The US 12 Heritage Route, stretching for 212 miles from New Buffalo on the west to Detroit, is the longest in Michigan. A unique fundraising initiative is the hosting and boasting of the longest garage sale in history, as people hawk their wares over the long course of the route. Heritage/cultural trails are often a work in progress because the level of development and visitor readiness varies along the way, and leaders see plenty of opportunity to improve the visitor experience. Located at the crossroads of US 12 and M-50, the Hewitt House at Walker Tavern is slated to become a gateway for this heritage route. Its location and the fact that it is a State of Michigan Historic Park make it ideally suited for this important role. "When the renovations and exhibits currently in the planning stages are complete, the Visitors Center will give guests an introduction to what the US 12 Heritage Trail has to offer, as well as an idea of what is was like to travel along this road in the past," explained Cheryl Natzmer Valentine, Walker Tavern historian. "Visitors will explore the answers to questions such as: who traveled the road at different times in history, why they traveled, and what they saw and did along the way. The story will be told through first-person travel narratives, artifact displays, and active learning activities that help visitors experience what travel was like in the past." To enhance the experience, trail coordinator, Kim Gallager, is exploring the potential of offering an audio/visual presentation that could be downloaded onto a mobile device.

The second example is Beachtowns, comprising nine communities along the west coast of Michigan, from New Buffalo to Ludington. The group has been a Travel Michigan regional marketing partner since 2001. "We are proud of the fact that Beachtowns is the oldest marketing partnership in the state, consistently generating more consumer visits to www.Michigan.org than any of the 24 other marketing partnerships currently working with Travel Michigan," stated Felicia Fairchild, chairperson of Beachtowns and executive director of the Saugatuck-Douglas Convention & Visitors Bureau. After receiving a national Preserve America grant, the organization partnered with the Michigan Historical Center to resurrect a highway designation from the past—the West Michigan Pike. Fairchild is very hopeful for what the development of a new heritage route could mean for this lake region. "In my opinion, we have just begun to demonstrate our potential. We are in the process of certifying Route 31 (the old West Michigan Pike) as an historic route, similar to Route 66, and will develop many marketing promotions around this lateral route in coming years. We are already collaborating with federal agencies to become part of the US 35 Bike Route, a coast-to-coast bike route which will run through the Beachtowns area." With matching funds, Travel Michigan provides a great opportunity for communities to dramatically affect their marketing impact.

Grand Haven's Beachtown promotion. Courtesy of Ed Post & Digital Active

A third illustration of a cultural heritage trail is the Iron Ore Heritage Trail in Marquette County where seven municipalities banded together to pass a ballot proposal to create a Recreation Authority. "Our vision for the Iron Ore Heritage Trail is to tell the 160-plus-year story of iron mining on the Marquette Range in an outdoor setting at the sites where the stories took place," said Carol Fulsher, administrator of the Recreation Authority. "In 2011, we should have approximately 30 miles of trail connecting the most populous areas in Marquette County. Not only are the communities now connected, but we have access to some amazing sites: many of the original mines of the 1840s; the plank road; the original forge; overlooks of the current mine operations; wetlands; Lake Superior's harbor and ore dock; and more." The passage of the Recreation Authority ballot proposal provides 2/10ths of a mill for six years and will generate $1.5 million in revenue for this trail development. This successful initiative demonstrates the value placed on the county's heritage, so much so that the electorate was willing to tax themselves to make it happen. It is a stunning example of cultural economic development. This heritage trail also capitalizes and connects significant existing historical assets—the Cliffs Shaft Mine Museum in Ishpeming and the Michigan Iron Industry Museum in Negaunee.

ECONOMIC INCENTIVES

Though private enterprise is the principal driver of our economy, there is strong agreement that government must encourage development by providing an economic climate conducive to growth. Tax structure is generally at the forefront of that consideration, but most believe that government must also provide incentives to encourage investment in new and expanding enterprises. Thus, in Michigan, we have or have had tax abatement provisions, Renaissance Zones, Smart Zones, Tax Increment Financing Authorities, Brownfield Redevelopment Authorities, and more. If government is going to financially stimulate investment, then it is reasonable that there be quantifiable outcomes or measures of economic impact—job creation being the most common expectation. If not in place, capital investment and the addition to the local tax base should also be desired economic outcomes. The major hurdle for cultural economic development is to convince traditional economic development professionals that jobs in the cultural sector are real jobs. The tourism industry in Michigan has fought that battle for years, with doubters insisting this sector only employed low paid part-time and seasonal workers. Now with the growing use of the term creative entrepreneurs to describe an expansive category of non-traditional and less understood jobs, the cultural sector is facing the same challenge of acceptance and legitimacy.

Our country's greatest competitive advantage resides in a capacity to produce innovative, unique, and leading-edge products. Creative ideas that are converted into new creative products originate from many sources, both large and small. The risk of failure is an inherent characteristic of an entrepreneurial enterprise, particularly one emanating from a micro start-up business; yet government incentives should be available for more than just a lead-pipe cinch. The creative class represents a well-spring of entrepreneurial spirit, imagination, and originality resulting

The Iron Ore Heritage Trail, Marquette County, Michigan. Courtesy of the Michigan Municipal League

in real jobs that matter. When first introduced to Facebook, I scratched my head asking, "What the heck is this all about?" Fast forward to, "Oh my, I wish my mind had been that inventive." Despite the undertow of reservation expressed here, there is a growing shift of opinion in the economic development world. The example of Monroe County receiving the first Clean Michigan grant for a cultural product—i.e., the River Raisin Battlefield—recognized that this development was destined to create jobs and provides some encouragement. There are many other examples throughout Michigan. "We think that at a minimum current economic incentives should incorporate arts and culture initiatives," states Bob Trezise. "Our most prime example is that we believe eligible activities of brownfield TIFs (Tax Increment Financing) should include public art. In other words, while capturing private dollars, many pay for public infrastructure like sidewalks and landscaping out front; why not also a piece of public art out front? As far as new tools go, we wonder aloud about a technique called Super TIFs. These highly concentrated areas in a downtown area capture all taxes, including income and sales tax, but could be used to support arts and culture projects within that specific area (arts incubator, a sculpture, a performing arts center)."

In order to truly legitimize the cultural sector's role in economic development and convince decision makers, we must demonstrate the economic outcomes of job creation, capital investment, and contribution to the local tax base. Despite a strong bias, I know that this sector can deliver on that hard sell. Secondly, to be convincing, the cultural sector must adopt a methodology to assess and document its economic impact. Multipliers have merit, but I am concerned that they are over-used, over-simplified, and they don't seem very empirical. A few years ago, the Michigan Department of History, Arts, and Libraries set out to address this felt need and engaged Michigan State University Professor Edward Mahoney, an economist, to develop an economic impact model for the cultural sector. With his staff, he created the Cultural Economic Development OnLine Tool (CEDOT). Although not yet implemented, this model incorporates a number of features that need to be seriously considered. There have been many thoughtful economic impact studies completed in the past, but each soon became outdated. CEDOT will be an online tool capable of providing information instantaneously, thereby insuring currency. Yes, it too uses a multiplier; how an organization determines its base data is critically important in producing numbers deemed to be valid measures. The formula requires the collection of zip codes to identify out-of-town visitors, length of stay, and the number of parties - not individuals – in order to compute the number of room nights. It then uses established and recognized spending profiles to generate direct spending of these visitors. Multipliers are used to determine indirect spending and tax revenue generated.

Quality of life is universally valued and cultural amenities play a major role in where we want to live. The new economy, or knowledge economy, will greatly influence the diversification that is surely to occur in Michigan. In the new economy we will witness an increasing recognition of the value of cultural assets and how they can be deployed to cause economic growth and community prosperity.

Dr. William Anderson was the founding director of the Michigan Department of History, Arts and Libraries, serving in the cabinets of Governors John Engler and Jennifer Granholm. The department carried the flag for cultural economic development encouraging cultural organizations and communities to strategically deploy their cultural resources to spur economic growth. Anderson has chaired numerous economic development organizations and facilitated the development strategic plans for many organizations. He is the author/editor of nine books.

federal urban policy: remedy or obstacle to michigan municipalities

JOHN NORQUIST

Michigan enjoyed prosperity even before it became a state in 1837. Its forests, natural resources, and position at the center of the Great Lakes gave it great advantages. Its industrial innovation produced great wealth that was used to create well-built cities like Detroit, Grand Rapids, Lansing, and Flint. In the last 40 years, decline set in and many manufacturing jobs were lost. Many of Michigan's municipalities have suffered decline in population and the tax base. While it may be tempting for some Michiganders to believe that this just happened like bad weather, it is important to try to understand and remedy policies that may have hastened decline. In this chapter, I examine federal policy and its impact on Michigan and its cities.

Since the Great Depression, municipal organizations like the U.S. Conference of Mayors and the National League of Cities have frequently called for a federal urban policy. By policy, they mean federal programs that benefit cities, particularly city governments. Revenue sharing, federal block grants, disaster relief, homeland security grants, energy grants, housing programs, and most recently stimulus funds are all programs that have provided cash to local governments. Some programs currently exist. Others have been cancelled. Revenue sharing, enacted under President Richard Nixon, was ended under President Reagan. While federal aid to cities is often discussed, it might surprise people to know that cities actually get little of their revenue from the federal government. In most years, it's less than 5 percent and the biggest share of that is assistance to public housing residents. The mostly unsuccessful effort to extract more money from the federal government should perhaps be replaced with an effort to remove obstacles that the federal government has placed in the way of urban development and redevelopment.

1954 - Packard's East Grand Boulevard plant, Detroit, Michigan. Courtesy of www.theoldmotor.com

KEY OBSTACLES

1) Traditionally, through the history of human civilization, streets have served three purposes in the urban context: the movement of people and goods; the conduct of commerce (the market place); and the social interaction of the community (Main Street). The U.S. Department of Transportation (DOT) and by extension state DOTs, however, classify streets almost exclusively by their "level of service," which reflects the street's performance on just one of these three key functions—movement. Narrower still, this functional classification system excludes considerations of how well streets serve pedestrians, bicycles, and transit service, and instead focuses solely on motor vehicle traffic. Since the system rates streets more highly for carrying more automobile and truck traffic regardless of impacts on the economic and social value of streets, federal and state funding flows to street designs that actively undermine the community's efforts to create valuable, livable, and sustainable communities. The goal of the federal road program is reducing automobile congestion. This is far too simple since congestion is much like cholesterol—congestion can be both good and bad. In sustainable communities with highly connected networks of walkable streets and transit, concentrations of people are signs of health, vitality, and outstanding environmental performance.

Federal funding also facilitates long trips and fails to account for the value of short-distance and non-motorized trips. In an economic and social sense, a person walking across a street to work at a job contributes as much as a person driving 25 miles to work at the same job. Federal policy should support economic value without disadvantaging compact, energy-efficient, transit-served urban development, as Harvard economics professor Edward Glaeser argued persuasively in the *Boston Globe* (March 9, 2010).

2) Federal housing policy disadvantages urban living by favoring home ownership over renting through subsidized mortgage programs—e.g., Fannie Mae, Freddie Mac, the Federal Housing Authority (FHA)—and by allowing tax deductions up to $2 million on mortgage interest. Also, Department of Housing and Urban Development's (HUD) 221 D4 capital subsidy for rental housing obstructs mixed-use development, including housing and retail, by prohibiting more than 20 percent of the imputed value of a project to be non-residential. Fannie Mae and Freddie Mac impose similar restrictions on owner-occupied housing. Potential buyers in a new four-story building with three floors of housing and shops on the ground floor would find it difficult or even impossible to secure mortgage financing because rules at Fannie Mae or Freddie Mac bar the mortgage giants from involvement in buildings where non-retail uses exceed 20 percent. Likewise, developers of either for-sale housing under Fannie and Freddie or rental housing under the 221 D4 program find it nearly impossible to get financing from banks, almost all of whom mimic and impose the federal restrictions on mixed-use.

A daily occurrence on U.S. highways. Courtesy of istockphoto.com/MCCAIG

Scale, building type, and financing—rent or mortgage—are the ingredients of a housing market that serves the varied needs of citizens. When federal programs are built around specialized concerns, they can obstruct the beneficial complexity of urban places. Financial requirements that dictate a separation of use or discourage rent-based housing work against the interests of diverse urban areas and the people who live in them. They also severely limit the ability to bring homes, schools, stores, offices, and other important destinations within walking distance—a pattern shown to yield dramatic benefits in energy efficiency, public health, household transportation costs, and environmental impact.

Midwest cities have especially suffered from federal and state programs and local policies that undermine urbanism and population density while subsidizing and encouraging decentralization—often referred to as sprawl. For example, the Interstate Highway program subsidizes grade-separated highways that facilitate fast long distance travel by motor vehicle. Connecting distant metros by express roads certainly holds benefits for travelers. Also, interstates hold a practical utility that makes great sense in rural areas with low costs per acre and few if any existing structures to remove. But in densely populated cities, roads are expensive, weaken property value, and disrupt the efficiency of existing street networks. The large grade separated highway undermines one of the fundamental assets of cities—location efficiency. If two people hold similar jobs and one person walks across the street to work, while the other drives 25 miles, their value to the economy is the same, but their cost is not. The government rewards the longer, energy-consuming trip with a large subsidy and ignores the value of the short walk. Federal policy should support economic value without disadvantaging compact, energy-efficient, transit-served urban development.

Billions of dollars being spent on infrastructure across the nation provide an opportunity to plan for a better America, but politics-as-usual favors sprawl over cities. This anti-urban bias of national policies must end.

Over the past 60 years, cities have been hit by a painful policy trifecta: subsidization of highways; subsidization of homeownership; and a school system that creates strong incentives for many parents to leave city borders. Nathaniel Baum-Snow, an economist at Brown University, has documented that each new federally funded "highway passing through a central city reduces its population by about 18 percent.'' Subsidizing transportation decreases the advantage of living close together in cities, which should make every urbanite worry about the Senate's fondness for using highway spending to fight recession.

The clear and often-stated goal of federal transportation policy is to reduce congestion. This narrowly focused objective clashes with the very purpose of cities as a gathering spot for commerce and cultural interaction. Let's face it, successful cities become congested because people choose to be in them. Cities, like New York, Chicago, and San Francisco, which have vibrant economies and high real estate values/square mile, experience congestion. However, it is not just traffic congestion, but also people, money, and job congestion. Cities like Detroit and Buffalo with shrinking economies and low real estate values have low congestion. They also may have low congestion because both cities are crisscrossed with freeways. In one way, the freeway building in Detroit and Buffalo has succeeded in achieving the stated goal of government policy, the American Association of State Highway and Transportation Officials' (AASHTO) Green Book, to reduce congestion. AASHTO uses a system that would rate Detroit quite highly.

These infill projects in Montgomery, AL (a) and Milwaukee, WI (b) on former surface parking lots feature housing in buildings that are more than 20 percent devoted to retail or commercial uses. Rules at Fannie Mae, Freddie Mac, and HUD discriminate against such projects, making development loans and individual mortgages difficult or impossible to obtain.

The Highway Capacity Manual and AASHTO Geometric Design of Highways and Streets ("Green Book") list the following levels of service:

A= Free flow
B=Reasonably free flow
C=Stable flow
D=Approaching unstable flow
E=Unstable flow
F=Forced or breakdown flow

By this measure, congestion is no longer much of a problem for Detroit. While cities like New York City and San Francisco suffer from congestion ratings at E and F, Detroit enjoys almost free flowing traffic. So, while federal and state transportation value low congestion, the market, as measured by real estate prices, values places with high levels of congestion.

Cities are beginning to understand that focusing narrowly on moving traffic on big roads is counterproductive. In 1975, New York City's West Side Highway fell down. The expressway, built in the 1930s, was literally at the end of its design life of 40 years. The elevated roadway blocked views of the Hudson River from Chelsea, Tribeca, and the Battery. The neighborhoods wanted their views back. They wanted to reconnect with the river. After a struggle that lasted more than a decade, the decision was made to replace the expressway with a surface thoroughfare, West Street. It paid off in higher real estate values, more development, and more jobs. Similarly, San Francisco and Portland eliminated freeways and gained population, jobs, and housing. In Milwaukee, we sought the elimination of the Park East Freeway on the north end of downtown. After a decade of struggle, we opened McKinley Boulevard in 2003. It replaced the freeway and is now a lucrative site for development. Manpower Inc., a Fortune 500 corporation, moved from the suburbs to a site adjacent to the boulevard. Thousands of new housing units have been added to the neighborhood and traffic distribution has actually improved without the freeway. Millions of dollars of development has occurred along the corridor. One cautionary note, Milwaukee County, which owned almost 90 percent of the land under the Park East Freeway, encumbered the right of way with "community benefits" restrictions on developers, contractors, and landowners that have slowed development in the right of way itself. Adjacent properties have surged in value, but the social restrictions have, in my opinion, been a drag on redevelopment.

Traffic that is just moving through cities—without visiting—holds little or no value for the city, while traffic that is moving to a destination within the city can hold great value. As I mentioned before, traffic congestion is a bit like cholesterol. There is both good and bad cholesterol and cholesterol levels need to be managed, not eliminated. Trying to defeat congestion without considering the nature of particular traffic, can generate collateral damage that can severely damage a city's vitality. Detroit and many other cities have removed on-street parking to free up room for through traffic. With the same objective, they have also converted two-way streets to one-ways. Both these actions hinder the ability of shoppers to conveniently visit downtown retailers. Streets like Gratiot and Jefferson should be the bustling centers of Detroit's commerce and civic life, but instead, they are mostly devoted to moving cars during Detroit's very brief commuter rush period. The threat of congestion was also addressed by the construction of three freeways

Manhattan Traffic, New York, New York. Courtesy of www.istockphoto.com/ VitaBella

through downtown Flint, a city of 111,000 people. Paris and London, by comparison, have about 10 million people and no freeways running through their centers. Interstates 69, 75, and 475 (the UAW Expressway) are clear examples of infrastructure serving the government's narrow-minded battle against congestion, even though there is little congestion to be concerned about.

To the Federal Highway Administration's credit, they have helped the Institute of Transportation Engineers and the Congress for the New Urbanism produce the Urban Context Street Guide. This manual provides guidance for engineers and planners who wish to build thoroughfares as avenues, boulevards, and streets instead of freeways and large arterials. It is available for free download at ite.org.

Another example of a policy that undermines urbanism is the application of strictly separated use zoning to cities. The federal government started promoting such zoning in 1931 in an Executive Order issued by President Herbert Hoover. Hoover, who had served as administrator of the U.S. relief effort to help a devastated Europe recover at the end of World War I, felt that U.S. cities, like those in Europe, were crowded and dirty and needed to spread out and separate commerce from housing. Although his order was more exhortatory than mandatory, its underlying intent remains embedded in many federally created policies and programs, including the two huge federal guaranteed secondary mortgage markets, Fannie Mae and Freddie Mac, as well as the Department of Housing and Urban Development's 21(d) capital subsidy program for multi-family rental housing. Separate use zoning has undermined the value of existing neighborhoods, and it had the effect of mandating new development be separated into pods with housing, retail, and office uses strictly separated. This confounds efforts to build a traditional Main Street with apartments built above storefronts.

Luxembourg architect/planner Leon Krier compares experiencing the traditional city to eating a delicious chocolate cake that is properly assembled from ingredients and carefully baked. He then describes U.S. style suburban sprawl like the ingredients of the cake—the sugar, water, cocoa, flour and baking powder—spread over the kitchen counter and then consumed separately. Not very tasty! It is, Krier says, the complexity, connectivity, and diversity of the properly assembled city that can be better enjoyed. Many federal and state policies have encouraged sprawl and undermined urbanism. But market and demographic forces, as described by Chris Leinberger, Urban Land Strategist and Developer, in his book *The Option of Urbanism: Investing in the American Dream*, have begun to favor urban places. As household sizes shrink, demand increases for urban forms such as apartments and town houses. Young adults prefer urban living, seeking greater social and job opportunities. Urbanism is more popular, so now would seem to be a good time to change rules and policies that discourage it.

In Milwaukee, as mayor from 1988 to 2004, I set out to reform coding and zoning to encourage mixed-uses in commercial and retail corridors. The code reforms adopted in Milwaukee "legalized" urban forms, like apartments or offices above shops. Also, setback requirements for buildings were adjusted to encourage construction of buildings along sidewalks and closer to streets. In newer portions of the city, setbacks from streets had been set as deep as 100 feet—often with no provision for sidewalks.

In some older portions of the city zoning, overlays had been imposed on commercial streets in the 1950s and 1960s that gave existing buildings non-conforming uses, thus making them condemnable for the purpose of eventually widening streets. This had the effect of undermining the ability of property owners to attract capital to repair or improve property, as banks and title insurance companies held no interest in assuming risk in property likely to face condemnation. For example, one of Milwaukee's east/west thoroughfares, National Avenue, is 54 feet wide—wide enough for two moving lanes in each direction, plus a lane on each side for parking. In 1962, the city council of Milwaukee, at the request of the Public Works Department, imposed a setback on the south side of the street that would create a travel surface of 72 feet, thus providing room for two additional lanes. If this policy had been carried to completion, three miles of buildings, collectively worth many millions of dollars, would have been removed to speed up traffic on National Avenue. Instead, we repealed the non-conforming use setback and legalized the avenue's existing dimensions.

Another counterproductive encumbrance on urban property is off-street parking regulation. Water Street runs along the west side of Milwaukee's city hall. In the early 1960s, off-street parking requirements were imposed on private property on Water. A building with a frontage of 19 feet had been lost to fire. The new ordinance required seven off-street parking spots on the lot, even though it was only 70 feet deep and the other buildings on the block were three and four stories. As a result, the lot sat vacant for 35 years until we relaxed the off-street parking requirement. A four story mixed-use building was constructed almost immediately after the change. Cities all over America have unnecessarily repressed their own real estate development with counterproductive parking requirements. Donald Shoup, a University of California Los Angeles economist, wrote a book about it titled, *The High Cost of Free Parking*. He discourages local officials from requiring parking, and instead urges them to leave that decision to property owners and their tenants. According to Shoup, most medium and large U.S. cities underprice on-street parking. They also not only have parking regulations that undermine the value of the city, but wastefully invest taxpayer funds on underutilized publicly owned parking.

All of these interventions—oversized streets, separated uses, and parking minimums—derive from an attitude that undervalues urbanism. Fortunately, the current markets do place a higher value on urbanism.

At the end of World War II, the U.S. was triumphant and undamaged by war. Many of the cities of Germany and Japan—Hamburg, Dresden, Berlin, Tokyo, Hiroshima, and Nagasaki—lay in near total ruin. America had won and Germany and Japan had lost. U.S. cities had produced much of the war material that fueled the Allied victory. No city was more productive on either side of the battle lines than Detroit, which produced tanks, jeeps, artillery, aircraft, ammunition, and firearms. At war's end, Detroit had nearly two million people, a vast streetcar system, quality housing, and a vibrant downtown. It was a well-planned city with the Woodward Plan, named for Augustus Woodward, which was modeled after the L'Enfant plan of Washington D.C. Its radiating streets carried motor vehicles and served as trunk routes for a vast streetcar system. After World War II, the plan was ignored and a system of freeways was built and the streetcars removed.

How did this work out for Detroit? Today, all the cities of Germany and Japan are rebuilt, while Detroit, having lost more than half its population, looks as though it was ground zero for World War II. Other industrial cities have also suffered—usually not to the extent of Detroit—enough to appear in dire need of repair. Pittsburgh, Buffalo, Gary, St. Louis, and Cleveland, all lost half their populations from 1950 to 2000, and many medium and small industrial cities shrank as well.

There are, of course, many reasons that U.S. cities deteriorated in the post World War II period. New technology, particularly the automobile, changed travel patterns in a way that undermined the supremacy of downtowns as centers of commerce. Also, as America gained prosperity, many citizens freely chose to enjoy their prosperity in larger houses on larger lots outside the city. Yet, a significant part of the decline of U.S. cities can be traced to U.S. transportation and housing policies that distorted markets and pushed decentralization far beyond where market forces alone would have taken it. The federal government, and by extension state governments, subsidized and otherwise encouraged, through regulation, non-urban forms of development.

While not a major source of discretionary revenue, the federal government has, from the nation's founding, had a powerful impact on cities both for good and ill. Perhaps the most beneficial federal contribution to cities is the U.S. Constitution, and especially the Bill of Rights. Individual freedom is important to the culture and economy of cities. Another great federal contribution to U.S. cities is the guarantee of free commerce among the states without restrictions or tariffs. In many other ways, the federal government has undermined cities. Changing these anti-urban rules and policies to allow or even encourage urbanism would only help cities.

More successful cities will, in turn, also help America. More compact, complete, and well-connected development will save energy and add efficiency to the American economy. Urbanism also brings social benefits to communities. As it says in the preamble to the Charter of the Congress for New Urbanism, "The Congress for the New Urbanism views disinvestment in central cities, the spread of placeless sprawl, increasing separation by race and income, environmental deterioration, loss of agricultural lands and wilderness, and the erosion of society's built heritage as one interrelated community-building challenge."

For cities, states, and certainly the federal government, it's the right time to address that challenge. Michigan has begun that process. The Michigan Municipal League, the states' universities, and foundations, are searching and finding ways to make progress. The Woodward Avenue project connecting downtown with Detroit's northwest side, the downtown revitalization in Grand Rapids, and many other efforts show promise. But efforts in Michigan need to be supported by removing federal obstacles like anti-urban rules for mortgage markets and anti-urban design requirements for federally supported pavement projects. With federal, state, and local governments strapped for cash, now is the time to change the rules so that federal regulations and investments add value to cities and the economy.

John Norquist is the president of Congress for the New Urbanism. His work promoting New Urbanism as an alternative to sprawl and antidote to sprawl's social and environmental problems draws on his experience as a big-city mayor and prominent participant in national discussions on urban design and school reform.

Norquist was the mayor of Milwaukee from 1988-2004. Under his leadership, Milwaukee experienced a decline in poverty, saw a boom in new downtown housing, and became a leading center of education and welfare reform. In naming Milwaukee America's Most-Underrated City in 2001, the Utne Reader said Norquist "understands what makes cities work as well as anyone in America." Governing magazine named him Public Official of the Year in 1998.

He is the author of The Wealth of Cities *(Addison-Wesley, 1998), and has taught courses in urban planning and development at the University of Chicago, Marquette University, and the University of Wisconsin-Milwaukee's School of Architecture and Urban Planning.*

about the michigan municipal league

BETTER COMMUNITIES. BETTER MICHIGAN.

Founded in 1899, the League is the one clear voice for communities. Through advocacy at the state and federal level, we proactively represent municipalities to help them sustain highly livable, desirable, and unique places within the state. We create and offer our members services and events that range from traditional to cutting edge. We help educate and inspire our members to remain focused on their passion for the area they represent. We support our members' efforts to create vibrant communities through the League's advocacy program, the Prosperity Agenda, and through the Center for 21st Century Communities, where we assist local officials in identifying, developing and implementing programs and strategies that will enhance the state's communities as thriving places. The League is intent on creating a better future; a Michigan that prospers once again.